Most men hit a moment that they feel like their spiritual growth stalls out. I remember when I hit that point too—several times. And eventually, we all will. And the one thing that helps is a simple guide. This book is that guide for men—it's a way to move forward.

VINCE MILLER
President, Resolute Men's Ministry and Bible Studies

Joe Barnard has a passion to help young Christian men become more spiritually fit and effective in their families and communities. His book has much insight and a lot of practical help toward that goal. What he desires is more potent servants of Christ, and anyone who aspires to be such a servant will profit much from reading his book.

DAVID LYLE JEFFREY
Distinguished Senior Fellow, Baylor Institute for Studies in Religion
Emeritus Distinguished Professor of Literature and the Humanities,
Baylor University, Waco, Texas

With so many books on discipleship being written, do men really need one more? Well, they do need a discipleship book that doesn't rehash much of the same content, which is why men would do well to pick this up. In many ways, this is unlike most discipleship books. It imparts passion (like most) and encourages leadership (also like most), but this book provides men with a clear direction that many seem to lack. I plan to get this in the hands of my friends and work through it together.

JOHN PERRITT
Director of Resources for Reformed Youth Ministries (rym.org)
Author of *Your Days Are Numbered, What Would Judas Do?, Time Out!,*
Insecure, & Mark: How Jesus Changes Everything

Virtually every evangelical church talks about discipleship or uses some form of 'disciple' in articulating their mission. I have found few, however, that are effectively engaging their men in the type of discipling that Joe discusses in his book. His assessment of the obstacles, and ways to truly establish discipling relationships is clear, concise, and compelling. Every church that seeks to actualize the Great Commission would be well-advised to give this book to all of their men.

JOE SMITH
President, Strengthening the Church

Joe Barnard begins this book saying he doesn't want to induce a yawn by treating the same subjects in the same, timeworn ways. He doesn't. *The Way Forward* is wise, learned, and biblical. You need this, as does the righteous men's movement rising throughout the world. Trust me. Get this and live it.

STEPHEN MANSFIELD
New York Times Bestselling Author of *Building Your Band of Brothers* and *The Character and Greatness of Winston Churchill: Hero in a Time of Crisis*

Jesus calls His followers to be disciples who make disciples. Men and women face similar and distinct challenges in obeying Christ's command. *The Way Forward* provides a fresh look at the obstacles and opportunities men face as they seek to be built up into the image of Christ.

J. GARRETT KELL
Pastor, Del Ray Baptist Church, Alexandria, Virginia

As a pastor with a great desire to build men for the body of Christ, I was thrilled to read Joe Barnard's book, *The Way Forward*. It is a very practical discipleship itinerary aimed at men, and in doing so addresses one of the great needs of our day. This book is packed full of gospel wisdom which edified me and will serve an individual Christian man or a church men's ministry. Buy it. Read it. Be transformed by it.

GAVIN PEACOCK
Former professional footballer
Director of International Outreach, The Council on Biblical Manhood and Womanhood

There are multiple resources on discipleship, but Joe Barnard, in *The Way Forward*, offers a simple 'survival guide' for men who know Jesus and want to take the next step in their spiritual journeys. This short and practical guidebook addresses problems men encounter (e.g., exhaustion, frustration, distraction) and offers meaningful and attainable solutions. These solutions are coupled with action plans that pave clear pathways to genuine growth in Christ.

KEN BOA
President of Reflections Ministries
author of several books including
Conformed to His Image and *Life in the Presence of God*

JOE
BARNARD

THE
WAY
FORWARD

A ROAD MAP
OF SPIRITUAL GROWTH
FOR MEN IN THE 21ST CENTURY

CHRISTIAN
FOCUS

Scripture quotations are from *The Holy Bible, English Standard Version*, copyright © 2001 by Crossway Bibles, a division of Good News Publishers. Used by permission. All rights reserved.

Scripture quotations marked (NIV) are taken from *The Holy Bible, New International Version*®, NIV® Copyright © 1973, 1978, 1984, 2011 by Biblica, Inc.™ Used by permission. All rights reserved worldwide.

Scripture quotations marked (KJV) are taken from *The King James Version*.

Copyright © Joe Barnard 2019

paperback ISBN 978-1-5271-0467-9
epub ISBN 978-1-5271-0510-2
mobi ISBN 978-1-5271-0511-9

10 9 8 7 6 5 4 3 2 1

Published in 2019
Reprinted in 2020
by
Christian Focus Publications Ltd,
Geanies House, Fearn, Ross-shire,
IV20 1TW, Scotland, Great Britain

www.christianfocus.com

Cover design by MOOSE77

Printed in the USA

CONTENTS

This book is dedicated to the young men that attend my Friday morning Bible study. Dan, Caleb, Jeromy, Arthur, Lawson, Darien, Matthew, and Ryan. May the Lord grant you all the wisdom and strength required to grow into mighty men of God (1 Chron. 11:10).

The Warning Label

◁ ◁ ◁ ◆ ◆ ◆ ▷ ▷ ▷

Writing a book on discipleship is like scripting a Western. The formula has been attempted so many times that I risk inducing a yawn simply by introducing the topic. As a child I can remember watching a tiger in a zoo cage pacing back and forth over the same terrain simply because there was no new area to explore. I pitied the tiger since evidently he had nothing better to do. A similar feeling often fills me when I see a new book being advertised on the topic of discipleship. Not only are there countless books written about discipleship, but there are countless books retracing paths that have already been traversed by older and wiser Christians. Personally, I prefer not to eat leftovers. Therefore, right now, before interest fades, I need to demonstrate why this book deserves a place—not only on your shelves—but in your hands. Here are four reasons.

First, this book is an itinerary, not a map. When lost, an itinerary is far more useful than a map. The problem with a map is that it can, at times, provide too much information. It gives a lot of data that might or *might not* be needed. An itinerary, on the other hand, is limited by relevance. An itinerary communicates three things: location, destination, and a route between.

This book is an itinerary *for discipleship*, not a map *of discipleship*. There are already a lot of comprehensive resources on discipleship available that lay out all of the Biblical theology, spiritual disciplines, and historical forms that encompass the subject. If men want an academic treatise, they should look elsewhere. This is more of a survival guide than an encyclopedia. This book is written to men who are frustrated and confused, men who want to get from A to B as directly as possible, without unnecessary detours and prolonged delays.

Second, this book avoids the crags that have wrecked fleets of books on discipleship. What are these perils? Allow me to mention five. *(1) Ideal portraits.* I love the Puritan sage Thomas Watson; however, the table of contents of his *Portrait of a Godly Man* reads like the kennel club rules for a show dog. Fear not! No attempt will be made to describe the perfection of holiness.[1] My focus will be on the ideal candidate *for maturity,* not on the ideal *of maturity.* There is a world of difference between describing a model apprentice and describing a model professional. This book is for apprentices.

(2) Oppressive lists. A book like *Disciplines of a Godly Man* deserves a prominent place on the bookshelf of every Christian man, but more as a reference than a route. To ask men to complete a spiritual ironman will guarantee that only the fiercest of type-A personalities will attempt the race. Men do not need to know about every possible action step; they need to know about the most important next step. My goal is to pave a simple path for

---

1. To me, at least, sketches of perfection are too often cutoff switches of motivation. Like the law, they do a wonderful job revealing sin; they are less potent when it comes to fueling change. In what follows I will try hard to guard the spiritual power lines of men.

normal Christian men, not to set up an obstacle course for the sanctimonious elite.

(3) Simplistic methods. Here preachers (like me) are repeat offenders. How many short term sermon series are marketed with the promise of producing spiritual leaders in a matter of six, eight, or ten weeks? Let's be honest: there are no methods or programs that ensure spiritual growth. A four-year seminary course might boast that graduates know Greek, Hebrew, and a lot about church history and church doctrine. However, they cannot guarantee any level of maturity among their alumni. The reason for this is that spiritual growth is the product of grace, not technique. There are no 'Top 7 Habits of Highly Effective Christians.' All believers must pursue what Eugene Peterson has called a long obedience in the same direction.

(4) Low bars. If fixating on perfection is a threat to discipleship, so is the opposite mistake of pardoning sloth.[2] I have heard more than one Christian leader talk about the goal of discipleship being to enable Christians to become self-feeders. Self-feeding is good, even necessary, to spiritual growth, just as self-feeding is basic to natural growth. Yet, I have never met a mother who limited her parenting aspirations to teaching a child how to use a fork and knife. Physically and spiritually, maturity consists of more than eating. A man whose only spiritual goal is to have a daily quiet time is a man who is naive regarding the substance and end of the

---

2.   James Schall reminds us that within classic Christian spirituality sloth is something more than laziness. It is 'a lethargy that prevents us from making the effort to look at what is really important in our lives or from taking any positive step that might make us aware of what we should know or do.' See *A Student's Guide to Liberal Learning* (Wilmington, ISI Books, 2000), p. 26.

Christian life. Men do not need an impossible bar, but they do need a high bar. All men need what Jim Collins, the apostle of modern management theory, calls a BHAG, a big-hairy-audacious-goal. Motivation suffers as much by having too small of a vision as by having too big of one.

(5) Therapeutic remedies. Discipleship requires more of us than downloading information. Transformation requires participating in communal practices, doing good works, avoiding temptation, exercising self-control, and taking risks of obedience and sacrifice. Mind and body must both be at work for the potential of grace to be realized in the life of a believer. The always perceptive Puritan divine, Thomas Brooks, makes the comment that Christians must always be bifocal in their vision: they must keep one eye on Christ, what He has done for them, and another on their responsibilities, what He calls them to do through His Spirit.[3] My aim will be to maintain the delicate balance that Brooks recommends, a tight walk of looking and doing, believing and obeying, abiding and practicing.

Here is a third reason to keep your hands on this book: this is the notebook of a fellow traveler, a guy who has been lost more than once, and who has taken notes regarding his repeated failures. This book is the product of a life quest. The Apostle Paul once confessed to a young Christian leader that he was the chief of sinners and that

---

3. Brooks says, 'It is a sad and dangerous thing to have two eyes to behold our dignity and privileges, and not one to see our duties and services. I should look with one eye upon the choice and excellent things that Christ has done for me … and I should look with the other eye upon those services and duties that the Scriptures require of those for whom Christ has done such blessed things.' Thomas Brooks, *Precious Remedies against Satan's Devices*, 1652, see Part 3, Device 4 (Kindle edition).

God had saved him as a specimen of grace. I feel something similar regarding discipleship. I will happily confess before the world that 'I am the chief of wanderers' and that God has repeatedly rescued me in order to indicate His patience in dealing with sheep who like to jump the fence. If I had to write a life narrative, the overarching theme would be distraction: catching a clear vision of the glory of Christ only shortly thereafter to be diverted on a rabbit trail. Twice God has used *The Shadow of the Almighty*, the biography of Jim Elliot, to force me to reckon with my foolishness. I will never forget being given a copy when I was seventeen years old. My experience of reading the book was like that of a child born in a dungeon who is brought out to see the sun for the very first time. I had never beheld such a glorious picture of godliness. With my whole heart, I pledged to pursue the character, faith, and spirit that shimmered from the life of Elliot.

But I didn't. I ended up sidetracked by thinking about athletics, academic honors, travel, life experience, success, fun, and eventually ministry. Finally, when I turned thirty I decided to re-read the book. Again it crushed me. I wept. There was the same sparkling path that I had seen over a decade before, but somehow playing in mud puddles had kept me from enjoying the beach. Good things had distracted me from the best thing. I pleaded with God not to allow me to repeat the same error a third time, at least not to the same degree.

So why am I writing this book? I am writing this book to help other guys like me get out of the wilderness. These pages are the notes of a man who has spent too much time doing figure eights in the desert when he could have been advancing toward the Promise Land. Hopefully, other men can learn from my mistakes.

Fourthly, keep reading because the driving motive for writing this book is not pride or vainglory, but brotherly sympathy. Why add another book to the ever-growing stack on discipleship? I have one excuse for doing so: if there were a thousand hospitals in a city and yet the dying were queuing on the street, no one would be considered a fool for going out and building yet another hospital. Across the English speaking world (the part I know) men are languishing and in desperate need of spiritual counsel. If I am adding yet another book to the pile already written on discipleship, I do so in view of the extent of the need, with the hope that, in God's Providence, this book might be the treatment needed to revive at least one faltering soul.

But if this book must pass the test of whether the reader is interested, the reader must also pass the test of whether this book is right for him. Not every medicine is for every patient. Not every book is for every reader. At the outset, let me be clear regarding who should *not* read this.

This book is not for non-Christians. Everything in this book assumes that a man professes faith, understands the gospel, is born again, and has the Holy Spirit residing within. No attempt will be made either to evangelize the lost or to provide self-help for the unbelieving. To attempt the Christian life without the Holy Spirit is every bit as ridiculous as attempting to drive a car without an engine. Only the Spirit of God can empower the Christian life, which means that only those truly born again are candidates for genuine spiritual growth.

Equally, this book is not for brand new Christians. No contractor builds a house by starting with the walls and the roof. First, a foundation is laid, and then the walls and roof are added. Readers must be aware that this book is for stage-two Christians, not stage-one. The book attempts to frame walls assuming that concrete has already been poured. Discipleship requires a firm understanding of the gospel and the basic doctrines of grace. Anyone who is unclear about these truths needs to put this book down and begin elsewhere.[4]

So, then, who is the intended audience? This book is for Christian men who know the gospel, who profess faith, who long for transformation, but who are frustrated by their lack of spiritual growth. If I were Gandalf the Grey, I would cast a spell on this book and have one condition required for anyone to open and read it. That requirement would be a painful dis-satisfaction regarding personal holiness and communion with God. Only men whose hearts were singed in the flames of spiritual hunger would be given access to the following pages.

The overarching aim of this book is to help men find the road that leads to spiritual maturity. In order to do this, we will follow a simple itinerary, one that will be familiar to a lot of men: problem, solution, and plan. Section one is a careful diagnosis of the multiple factors that combine to stifle the spiritual growth of men. Too often men are given simplistic accounts for why they struggle (e.g. laziness, apathy, inability to prioritize, etc.). The truth is that men struggle for a lot of different reasons. Understanding the nature of an ailment is an important first step toward arriving at a cure. Section two is a description of the solution. If the aim of section one is for

---

4. Two books that do a wonderful job pouring the concrete of grace are Tim Keller, *The Prodigal God: Recovering the Heart of the Christian Faith* (New York: Riverhead Books, 2011) and Jerry Bridges, *The Gospel for Real Life* (Colorado Springs: NavPress, 2002).

a man to think to himself, 'Yes, that's me; that's why I struggle,' the aim of section two is for the same man to think, 'Yes, that's where I need to be; that would make the difference.' Section three outlines a plan. There is nothing crueler than helping a person understand a problem without then giving him assistance to overcome it. I hope to avoid all cruelty. The book will end with practical advice on the way forward. No method or technique will be offered. I am averse to anything that promises more than it can deliver. Therefore, the final section will be more akin to the advice that one traveler gives another than a definitive plan guaranteeing growth.

My hope throughout is to keep a brisk pace along a clearly marked path. Clarity, brevity, pertinence, application, and, most importantly, truthfulness – these are my goals in writing.

PART 1

The Problem

◁◁◁◆◆▷▷▷

Where are the Bananas?

In South Louisiana, where I grew up, banana trees are a familiar sight. They shade pool-side patios, decorate parking lots, and dot the lawns of neighborhood houses. I will never forget the excitement I felt as a child the first time I realized that trees producing one of my favorite foods were growing just outside my bedroom window. The enthusiasm soon wilted to disappointment, however. Over the next months I watched aghast as the fruit on the trees never ripened into edible form. I recall the frustration I felt as I observed the little clusters of fruit turn from green to black without becoming yellow. In South Louisiana, I discovered, bananas mature, but only so far. Their growth is stunted by a climate that is just warm enough to allow banana trees to grow, but too cold to permit fruit to ripen.

This childhood observation has become for me a parable by which I interpret the condition of Christian men. Time and again I have seen men profess faith in Christ, learn the rudiments of practical Christianity, and then mysteriously *stall*. They stop maturing. Five, ten, or twenty years into their walk with Christ they are in a condition similar to a year or two after their conversion.[1] A junior high science teacher was able to help me resolve the mystery of the banana trees. I have had a lot more difficulty figuring out an explanation for Christian men.

Early in my ministry I was surprised and frustrated by the slow development of men. I placed all of the blame on the shoulders of the guys in the pew. The individual man – he was the problem. An injection of self-discipline – that was the remedy. While I retain a hearty appreciation for self-discipline, after prolonged reflection, and a little bit more experience with men, my perspective has broadened. Today when I think of Christian men I associate them with the 'the replacements' of WWII. The first wave of soldiers who stormed Europe and North Africa were seasoned by meticulous training and focused preparation. Insofar as any soldier can be, they were combat ready. Yet, as this first group was depleted in number due to death, sickness, and injury, the guys who filled their foxholes were in many cases young, inexperienced, and untrained. Some were mere boys, barely able to use a razor, much less a rifle. Sadly, many of these replacements became unnecessary casualties of war. They could have performed better had they been trained properly.

I believe something similar is true of Christian men today. Guys who are spiritual newborns are left to care for themselves as if they were orphans. Lacking the knowledge, skills, and relationships which are vital to spiritual development, they never

---

1. This problem of stunted growth is not new. Spurgeon makes the following observation in his autobiography, 'I have often thought that if a man does not become a high class Christian during the first three months after his conversion he probably never will.'

mature into competent spiritual adults. Christians are not acorns that can fall into the soil and, with a little sun and water, grow into mighty oaks. Christians are infants that require faithful love and diligent care to nurture them toward maturity. Tragically, such 'spiritual parenting' is deficient for a lot of Christian men. Too many end up like the banana trees of South Louisiana, trapped in an adverse climate just warm enough to permit survival, but too cold to grow fruit.

An accurate diagnosis is always the first step to an effective remedy. In view of this, the aim of this section is to help men understand why they are struggling. Men are accustomed to hearing simplistic indictments from the pulpit. Preachers (like me) fire arrows toward the back seats, telling guys that if they would try harder, do more, or commit wholeheartedly, then maturity could happen. Most guys are sharp enough to know that this message is inadequate. They know that the problem is more complicated than a shortage of willpower. Indeed it is. When speaking to an obese patient, only the most careless of physicians would offer the knee-jerk advice *eat less*. Obesity is usually the result of multiple factors. Hormones, genes, psychology, inherited habits, poor education, environment, and, yes, insufficient self-control weave together like a spider's web to trap an individual.

The difficulty of diagnosing the feeble spiritual growth of a Christian man is no less difficult than figuring out why a man is out of shape. There is not a single cause leading to the problem; there are many. There is a surface to the predicament as well as a depth. Only by looking from multiple angles can the situation be fully understood. Keeping this in mind, we will look at seven factors that contribute to the stunted spiritual growth of men. The purpose of this will not be to compound guilt (though godly sorrow might be a good thing), but to enable understanding. Ultimately, my goal is to pave a way forward; however, the plan, which comes later, will only be compelling if the diagnosis is convincing.

The Surface

◁◁◁◆◆◆▷▷▷

The first tremor that shifted how I viewed the spiritual plight of men occurred while reading Matthew 9:35-38. In this passage Jesus is preaching, teaching, and healing people of their illnesses. Unexpectedly, the narrative zooms into the inner workings of Jesus' heart. Matthew writes, 'When he saw the crowds, he had compassion for them, because they were harassed and helpless, like sheep without a shepherd' (v. 36). *Harassed* and *helpless* – those two words shook me like thunder and lightning. I realized that Jesus was doing something that I had neglected: He was recognizing that there were multiple aspects to why the people around Him were spiritually impoverished. Did they have a deep and sinister sin problem? Yes, they did. But there was more than this. The people were like agitated sheep suffering from inadequate leadership. They had not been fed properly. They were unprotected. Their condition called for both the righteous zeal of a prophet and the tender mercy of a physician. Personally, I knew that zeal, in my case, had snuffed the warmth of mercy.

In what follows I want to look at five 'surface' aspects for why men aren't growing. I label these 'surface' for two reasons. On the one hand, I want to recognize that they are significant factors hindering the maturity of men. Yet, on the other, I also want to separate them from deeper issues that are even more fundamental in terms of diagnosing the roots of the problem.

Men are Exhausted

Exhaustion is often misdiagnosed as laziness. Human beings only have a certain measure of energy. Even factoring supernatural grace into the equation, grace is only supplied for God-appointed tasks, which means that Christian men are not a race of superheroes. They are not able to memorize the Bible, build soup kitchens, evangelize the lost, run marathons, and travel the world, all the while pursuing demanding careers. This point, which ought to be obvious, needs to be highlighted because of the cult of busyness that is characteristic of the modern world. The truth is that a lot of Christian men are attempting to complete insufferable task lists.[2] They are exhausting themselves to death. Three factors explain why this is the case.

First, Christian men feel the burden of fulfilling all of the demands of 'normal', modern life. Like non-Christians, we must work a job, maintain a house, pay taxes, cut the grass, and try not to forget about Valentine's Day. In this, our experience is no different than our dads and grand-dads. Yet, contemporary men shoulder additional burdens that our forefathers could not fathom. Take fatherhood, for example. Being a dad fifty years ago was a matter of patting little Johnny on the head, asking how school went, and then sending him out the door to play baseball with his friends. Parenting was a low-impact sport.[3] Modern fatherhood is radically

---

2. A lot of men today are task list junkies. Getting Things Done, the well-known GTD method of David Allen, has become for many a religion with productivity replacing holiness as the end goal.

3. Robert Putnam gives a helpful analysis of what he calls 'intensive

different. Today, a 'good' dad is a part-time Uber driver, an evening tutor, and a weekend event-planner. His parenting responsibilities include shuttling children from sports practices to violin lessons, building Ivy League résumés, and organizing activities lest 'Johnny' experience the greatest evil of all, *boredom.*

Yet, all of this is just the tip of the iceberg. A man is more than a dad. Outside of family, men feel the pressure to fulfill all the soft requirements of a reputable, middle-class existence, which include intensive workouts, fluency in current events (especially sports), regular doses of fun, and illustrious success in a notable profession. Thus by the time men hit middle age they physically have no bandwidth left. Coffee grinds can only carry them so far. At the end of a typical day, all spiritual duties excluded, men are toast. They barely have enough energy to find the TV remote, much less to open their Bibles and do a keyword study.

But there is more. On top of the 'secular' duties that men generally bear, Christian men must also shoulder the demands of modern churches. Few tyrannies are more oppressive than the expectations of a 'missional' church.[4] Walking through the doors of a lot of churches is eerily similar to getting caught in the gravitational force of a black hole. Churches zealously collect as

---

parentings' in *Our Kids: the American Dream in Crisis* (New York: Simon & Schuster, 2015), chapter 3.

4.   In saying this I am not opposed to missional churches. I love missional churches and fervently believe that every pastor should read the books of Steve Timmis and Tim Chester. The problem occurs when the selfish ambition of a pastor distracts from the actual mission of God's people. To be truly missional, pastors need to align their churches with God's agenda. For a useful description of this agenda, see Christopher Wright's book, *The Mission of God's People: a Biblical Theology of the Church's Mission* (New York: Harper Collins, 2010).

much data as possible—your name, address, phone number, and email—not so much to find out how visitors are doing spiritually, but to make sure that kids are signed up for children's programs, wives are bringing dishes to pot lucks, and men are chaperoning for junior high lock-ins. All of this might be acceptable if the assignments given fit within a larger vision of personal vocation. But too often the 'vision' of the leadership team eclipses any other purpose. Christians wind up feeling like factory workers being sacrificed for their productive energy rather than players being coached so that they can take the field and advance the ball for God. The point to glean from this is that a lot of men are doubly exhausted because they are trying to fulfill the 'spiritual' duties of church membership over and above the 'secular' duties of everyday living. No wonder they are tired.

Still, a third weight must be added to the barbell. There is no denying that Christ makes certain demands of His disciples. There is such a thing as a spiritual 'duty'. Christians must meditate on the Word (Josh. 1:8; Ps. 1; Col. 3:16 et al.). We must commit ourselves to prayer (1 Thess. 5:16). We must shepherd our children and love our spouses (Deut. 6; Eph. 5). We must work hard, earn our keep, and be charitable toward others (1 Thess. 3:6-15). Sin must be mortified; character cultivated; good deeds performed (Titus 2:14). Recognizing this, the ever-faithful Puritan Thomas Watson notes, 'It is not so easy a thing as men believe to get to heaven. There are so many precepts to obey, promises to believe, so many rocks to avoid, that it is a difficult matter to be saved.'[5] Watson was not innovating when he wrote this. He was simply

---

5. Thomas Watson, *The Christian Soldier*, 1670, see Part 8 (Kindle edition).

casting Jesus' teaching in a fresh mold: 'For the gate is narrow and the way is hard that leads to life, and those who find it are few' (Matt. 7:14).

So why are men exhausted? The answer is because they carry the compounded weight of the cultural expectations of the world around them, the missional expectations of ambitious church leaders, and the gospel expectations of Jesus Christ, their Lord and Savior. The combination of these is the straw (or rather straw-bale) that breaks the camel's back. Jesus promised His followers that His 'yoke is easy and his burden is light' (Matt. 11:30). Yet, there was an unspoken condition attached to the promise – that His followers would not doubly or trebly yoke themselves.

For many years I preached sermons with the subtext 'stop being lazy'. But one day I looked out and realized that, while there are some guys who are inert, a lot of others are industrious, hardworking, and self-disciplined. The problem with the latter was not indolence, but that they had bought into one of the great myths of our society: that life is a buffet at which you can have whatever you want.[6] This is a lie. Men cannot climb the corporate ladder, coach traveling soccer teams, visit all the national parks, teach Sunday school, get a black belt in jujitsu, and become mature spiritual leaders. Eventually, exhaustion becomes an insurmountable constraint and something gives. Sadly, for a lot of guys what gives is the closeness of their walk with God.

---

6. Anne Marie Slaughter has written a recent book demonstrating how the contemporary load of responsibilities shouldered by women is impossible to bear. Someone needs to write the companion volume—from a Christian perspective—for men. See Anne Marie Slaughter, *Unfinished Business: Women, Men, Work, Family* (New York: Random House, 2016).

Men are Frustrated

In the influential book *Switch*, Chip and Dan Heath make the point that what often looks like resistance is a lack of clarity.[7] Their insight might be rephrased as follows: what often looks like resistance is frustration, especially the frustration that comes from inadequate training. In observing men I have repeatedly watched as three different sources of frustration merge to sink spiritual motivation.

The first is the frustration of incompetence. As a teenager I was asked to paint the outside of a house. I was given all of the tools required. I had scrapers, sandpaper, caulk, brushes, and paint. However, I remember sitting as if paralyzed, wanting to dig a hole and hide. What was wrong? Was the problem that I was stubborn, rebellious, and unwilling? I don't remember feeling that way. Was the problem that I was lazy and resistant to being outside of air-conditioning under the hot summer sun? No. The problem was anxiety: I didn't know where to begin or what to do. I had never painted the exterior of a house before. No one offered me any instruction. What looked like resistance was in fact a petrifying awareness of incompetence.

I am convinced that one reason guys are spiritually stagnant is that a lot of men are in a position not unlike me when I was standing in front of a house, holding a paintbrush and a can of paint, but utterly ignorant of where to begin. Guys are told that they ought to be spiritual leaders in the home, prayer warriors, apt to teach, evangelists, apologists, disciple-makers, and mentors.

---

7. Chip and Dan Heath, *Switch: How to Change Things When Change Is Hard* (New York: Random House, 2010).

But these statements often incapacitate rather than inspire. No one 'shrinks the change' so that Christian men have a clear and simple path to follow.[8] As a consequence, some guys flee to the nearest driving range or hide behind a lawn mower because their spiritual calling sounds like a feat that requires an advanced graduate degree to perform.

This sense of incompetence can verge into despair. Christian men can feel as if spiritual growth is not only difficult, but impossible. As a teenager I had no doubts that painting a house was a task that could be accomplished, indeed something that many men could do with ease. The problem was that I was untrained. I knew that if someone would give me a little guidance the emotional knot would be undone. The frustration of despair is of a different order than this. A couple of years ago my kids enjoyed watching a TV show called *Beastmaster*. 'The Beast' was a giant obstacle course that required extreme fitness to be able to complete. In fact, even super-athletes were not guaranteed to be able to finish. Most, in fact, could not get through the preliminary obstacles. Too often the Christian life is presented to men as if it were 'The Beast', a giant obstacle course that only the few, the proud, the Marine Corps of Christians should attempt. Sermon after sermon piles on additional

---

8. The Heath brothers use the term 'shrink the change' to denote reducing what appears to be an impossible problem into what appears to be a manageable set of steps. See *Switch,* chapter 6. Dawson Trotman was particularly conscientious of this human need. Early in his ministry he observed: 'Human nature tends toward inertia in spiritual things and needs a prop, a stimulant – the stimulant of other persons to prod and encourage them to continue, and the convenience of methods which make as easy as possible to follow through.' Betty Lee Skinner, *Daws: the Story of Dawson Trotman* (Grand Rapids: Zondervan, 1974), p. 38.

duties, responsibilities, and roles to be performed. The net result is that men feel vertigo as they stare at a sheer face that no amount of training could enable them to climb.

Then there is a third rivulet feeding into the frustration of men. This is the frustration of pointless activities. Just as people need to know what to do and how to do it, they also need to know *why* a task is important. The maxim is undeniable: actions without ends feel unimportant. As a child I spent several years being taught classical piano. My teacher drilled me in scales, chords, and incrementally more difficult pieces of music. She was quite pleased with my progress. However, I quickly lost interest. Now I need to shoulder most of the blame for why I am not a proficient pianist today. (I could have practiced Beethoven more and basketball less). Nonetheless, among the reasons is the fact that my teacher never explained to me why I had to endure a hamster wheel of technical exercises. She never taught me basic theory or presented me with a compelling vision of graduating into musicianship. I was like Daniel in *The Karate Kid*, endlessly waxing cars and painting fences, except, in my case, Mr Miyagi never explained how simple motions connected with whipping bullies.

A lot of guys have a similar experience spiritually. Through churches and Bible studies they are told a long list of spiritual disciplines, the stuff a godly man is supposed to be doing *all of the time*. But, for many guys, these exercises are never framed within a holistic vision of the Christian life. Hence, detached from worthy aims and objectives, such disciplines feel as exciting as another twenty minutes on the treadmill. Quiet times, intercessory prayer, Scripture memorization, and the full gamut of other activities are like the boulder of Sisyphus that had to be pushed up a hill one day only to roll back down so that the task could be repeated the next day.

Like laziness, I used to be quick to denounce the general apathy of men for spiritual activities. My diagnosis is now less whimsical. Are there apathetic Christians? Of course. Many do nothing because they have forsaken their first love. Yet, I now cast this charge cautiously, only after other potential conditions have been ruled out. I know from experience that there are men slumped over in pews who deeply hunger for growth but who are frustrated due to being handed a job description that would frighten the most earnest of monks. Jesus' indictment against the religious leaders of His day is equally pertinent to our own: 'They tie up heavy burdens, hard to bear, and lay them on people's shoulders, but they themselves are not willing to move them with their finger' (Matt. 23:4).

Men are Alone

In 1947 S.L.A. 'Slam' Marshall published a book called *Men against Fire*[9] that jarred military leadership. Marshall was a veteran of WWI and a military historian who, during WWII, interviewed thousands of men regarding their experience of combat. His basic conclusion was that the average man's experience of battle was strikingly different from what he had expected. Men knew that combat would be frightening and that it would test the full resources of their mental, emotional, and physical energy. But battle, thought they, would be a kind of amped up version of a high school football game. Adrenalin would surge, a spirit of camaraderie would

---

9. S.L.A. Marshall, *Men against Fire: the Problem of Battle Command* (Norman, University of Oklahoma Press, 2012.)

prevail, and a sense of duty would make up for a deficit of strength and courage. That was, at least, how Hollywood had presented war.

What men actually experienced was nothing like this. At the first sound of enemy fire all soldiers immediately dropped to the ground losing sight and communication with fellow comrades. Suddenly, the individual soldier felt horrifyingly alone and uncontrollably afraid. Whereas he had expected the enemy to be a plain target, in fact, the enemy was equally scared and therefore equally hidden. The most controversial aspect of Marshall's book was his claim that, on average, only one in four soldiers ended up firing his weapon. The rest were too shocked, afraid, and *alone* to be of much tactical use.

Regardless of the merit of Marshall's research, his description of men on the battlefield is a useful image for understanding the experience of Christian men as they seek to honor Christ in the real world. A lot of men expect the work of the devil to be obvious. They think that their inner resolve will be sufficient to keep them on the right track in the face of difficulties. They assume that their relationships with other Christians are strong enough to support them through suffering and temptation. They are like the first wave of British soldiers at the Somme who happily climbed out of their trenches thinking that the battle was under control.[10] A lot of guys never foresee the degree to which weakness, fear, anxiety, and loneliness will grip them in the midst of affliction and leave them paralyzed or desiring to flee the frontline.

---

10. John Keegan's terrifying description of the battle of the Somme can be read as a parable of how not to engage in spiritual combat. See John Keegan, *The Face of Battle: a Study of Agincourt, Waterloo, and the Somme* (New York: Penguin, 1983), ch. 4.

This naivety is why a lot of men do not invest in spiritual friendship. During comfortable phases of life, friendship feels like a luxury. 'I can manage on my own' is the unspoken conviction of men when skies are fair. But like the North Sea the conditions of life can change rapidly. A crisis strikes and suddenly men discover that no one knows them well enough to be of help. Or, just as pernicious, a more subtle drift occurs so that a man follows the deceitfulness of sin without there being anyone close enough to deliver a much needed rebuke. The consequences of this isolation can be devastating. Like people climbing out of the rubble after an earthquake, a lot of men wake up in their late forties to the realization that that their wife is gone, their kids hate them, and that the BMW in the garage doesn't fill the void. They are like drivers who have driven through the night not realizing a wrong turn was taken 500 miles back. If they had had someone in the passenger seat, the error might have been detected.

The question is worth asking why spiritual isolation is such a widespread problem for men in the church. A part of the answer is poor leadership. While there are endless programs and events organized for men via churches and parachurch ministries, there is very little direct teaching on the topic of spiritual friendship. For some reason pastors and other Christian leaders assume that men know (1) what Christian friendship is and (2) that Christian friendship is not an amenity but a necessity to discipleship. The old lesson from Aristotle is forgotten that there are multiple forms of friendship and that not every form is of equal worth. Thus churches continue to provide men with book studies and breakfasts unaware that an underlying need for spiritual camaraderie persists unacknowledged and therefore unmet.

But there is a further assumption made by pastors and church leaders that is equally dangerous. This is that community groups satisfy the needs of Christians for intimacy, accountability, and encouragement. The truth is that they do not and cannot. There are temptations and sins that can only be confessed in a narrow and tightly secured circle of trust. There is accountability and support that can only be provided by relationships that have weathered years, even decades. Do men need small groups for fellowship and support? Yes, they do. But the diet of large group worship balanced by small group fellowship is insufficient to produce strong and healthy men. In addition to these, men need a spiritual band of brothers who will provide support and accountability as outlined in Ecclesiastes 4:

> *Two are better than one,*
> *Because they have a good return for their labor:*
> *If either of them falls down,*
> *One can help the other up.*
> *But pity anyone who falls*
> *And has no one to help them up.*
> *Also, if two lie down together, they will keep warm.*
> *But how can one keep warm alone?*
> *Though one may be overpowered,*
> *Two can defend themselves.*
> *A cord of three strands is not quickly broken.* (Eccles. 4:9-12)

Interestingly, one of the chief recommendations of Marshall was to reorganize fighting units around what he called 'fire-teams'. A fire-team consisted of a handful of soldiers who were careful to maintain communication and to protect each other's backs. If set within such a group, men who otherwise hid from the face of battle found strength and courage to fulfill their assignments. Christians ought to ponder the spiritual implications of this observation.[11]

Men are Nearsighted

We all know what it means to be nearsighted. Nearsightedness is when the stuff right in front of you is plain and visible but anything in the distance is fuzzy and indecipherable. There are many practical disadvantages that come with nearsightedness. Limited vision can cause missed opportunity. Not to see something is to overlook (or rather *underlook*) a possibility. Consider an extreme example. Imagine a nearsighted man who is stranded on a raft in the middle of the ocean. There is a boat on the horizon passing him by, but he does not see the boat, and therefore makes no attempt to get its attention. The example might appear laughable due to the rarity of being stranded on open waters. However, there is physical nearsightedness and spiritual nearsightedness, and the consequences of weak spiritual vision are even worse than missing a rescue boat.

There is no denying that the Christian life depends upon a long-term perspective, the ability to see not only what is at hand but also what is at the edge of life – eternity. Nothing is more uniquely Christian than hope, and hope is essentially holding fast to something that is not yet fully given.[12] As Christians, we

---

11. Marshall says, 'I hold it to be one of the simplest truths of war that the thing which enables an infantry soldier to keep going with his weapons is the near presence or the presumed presence of a comrade.' Marshall, *Men against Fire*, p. 42.

12. Two provocative works on Christian hope are Tom Wright, *Surprised by Hope: Rethinking Heaven, the Resurrection, and the Mission of the Church* (New York: HarperOne, 2009) and Saint Augustine's classic, *The Enchiridion*.

hope for a bodily resurrection even while we observe our bodies weakening, decaying, and ultimately being buried or cremated. We hope for rewards in heaven (things we cannot see) while sacrificing pleasures, comforts, and honors on earth (things we can see). We hope for justice, righteousness, and happiness even though we often feel the need with Job to exclaim: 'The thing that I have feared has come upon me' (3:25). Nothing is more basic to Christianity than the need to live by faith, not sight, which is to say by long-term, not short-term vision.

One reason why Christian men are stunted in their growth is that their vision is skewed. They are spiritually nearsighted. This nearsightedness can take two forms. The first is the nearsightedness of King David. Most of us will be familiar with the story of how David, one of the great men in the Bible committed a grievous sin against God. He saw a beautiful woman bathing on the rooftop beside his palace, got her pregnant, and then, trying to avoid the consequences of public humiliation, organized the murder of a good friend who also happened to be the woman's husband. But the full tragedy of the scene is only evident once Nathan the prophet shows up and reveals just how limited David's perspective was when he chose momentary pleasure over enduring righteousness. Nathan, speaking on behalf of God, says, 'I gave your master's house to you, and your master's wives into your arms. I gave you all Israel and Judah. And if all this had been too little, I would have given you even more' (2 Sam. 12:8 NIV). Those last seven words are harrowing: *I would have given you even more*. What David lost sight of while lured by lust was the reality that the fullness of joy was not in the arms of a woman but at God's right hand (Ps. 16:11). God could have—indeed would have—provided David with far more joy, and better joy, than any guilt-infused affair could supply. Yet, sadly, the sun was eclipsed by a candle, and David chose a one-night stand over an abiding communion with God.

The nearsightedness of David is a common ailment among men. The pleasures, comforts, and honors of the world are constantly on display. Modern society is institutionally structured to make sure that instant gratification is affordable and available to all. Meanwhile the great goods, the fine vintages of personal knowledge of God, genuine spiritual-fulfillment, and eternal rewards, are hidden in a cellar out of view. Richard Baxter, in his classic *The Saints' Everlasting Rest*, makes the comment, 'When God would give the Israelites his Sabbaths of rest, in a land of rest, it was harder to make them believe it, than to overcome their enemies, and procure it for them.' This difficulty of belief is, for many, a difficulty of sight. A lot of men order a peanut butter and jelly sandwich because they do not see the ribeye steak on the menu. They settle for less because they forget that there is more.

The other form of nearsightedness that plagues men is that of Alexander the Great. The story is well known that, after having conquered parts of India, Alexander wept because there was no more land to conquer. This has often been read as a sign of the heroic spirit of Alexander. In truth, the tears are a symptom of naivety. The grief deserves a good belly laugh. There is no need to diminish the exploits of the illustrious Greek general. He completed one of the most extensive and brilliant military campaigns in all of human history. But poor Alexander suffered from a lack of perspective. His tear-ridden eyes blinded him from the wide expanse of territory that was available for further conquest. After all, he could have taken his army south into the continent of Africa; he could have moved east and invaded China; he could have ventured north toward Russia; and, if all of this was not enough, there were two gigantic continents across the Atlantic waiting to be 'discovered'. All this to say that Alexander's tears were premature. He felt that the work had been completed when in truth it had only just begun.

Like David, Alexander casts a light into the hearts of men. One does not need to search far in churches to find men who have spiritually settled in life because they overestimate their maturity. One of the greatest dangers of earnest Christians is to judge their spiritual condition by the standards of those around them. Several years ago, in Scotland, I decided to start taking my two boys to a swimming pool at a fitness club in order to teach them to swim. Being in the thick of family life and pastoral ministry, I had taken a long sabbatical from working out. I remember stepping into the swimming pool, looking at the other dads, and feeling a spirit of self-congratulation that in spite of being so busy I had remained fit. About three weeks later I decided to start using the weight room at the same club. I'll never forget walking through the doors for the first time and laughing as I realized that the average fitness in a weight room is a little higher than in a public swimming pool. At the swimming pool, fitness was defined by a comparatively trim waistline. In the weight room, being 'in shape' required muscle definition and stamina. I learned that day the danger of boosting my pride by means of an inaccurate measure.

I often hear older Christian men reminisce about the early days of faith when they participated in in-depth Bible studies, memorized reels of Scripture, relished spiritual fellowship with other believers, and readily shared their faith with non-Christians. Although the point is rarely stated plainly, assumed in these conversations is the idea that, somewhere along the way, these activities stopped and that early fervor cooled into easy contentment. The experience is common. Why does it happen? One reason is that the spiritual vision of men is truncated. Once a guy gets a little ahead of the pack, like the hare in Aesop's well-known fable, he feels as if the pace can be slackened. Christians begin to measure their progress by the average rather than the end goal. Like me at the swimming pool, they begin to high five themselves and self-congratulate. They repeat the blunder of Alexander and begin to think that they can retire to leisure because there is no more ground to conquer.

There are few hazards more dangerous to Christians than thinking that they have arrived at the heights of godliness when in fact they are in the foothills. Although few men would publicly profess to be emblems of discipleship, many feel this way. They are like Terah who settled midway to the Promised Land because he did not understand the full extent of the itinerary (see Gen. 11:31-32). Such men need corrective vision. They need to appreciate that progress is best measured, not by how far we have come, but by how far we are summoned to go. Such perspective is vital for killing off the roots of pride and for maintaining an ongoing supply of spiritual initiative.

Men are Distracted

We live in an attention economy. Modern companies view our attention as a finite resource every bit as valuable as crude oil or natural gas. In view of this, the effort to capture our attention at home, at work, or in-between has become every bit as fierce and competitive as the Oklahoma land rushes of the nineteenth century.

The novelty of this situation is worth noting. In the book *Attention Merchants*[13] Tim Wu tells the story of Benjamin Day, the founder of the *New York Sun*, the first penny newspaper. Before Benjamin Day conceived of the *Sun*, newspapers were too expensive for a mass market, and they focused on presenting the beliefs of the writers rather than feeding the interests of the readers. Day had a radical idea. He was the first to recognize that people's attention could itself be viewed as a commodity. This insight led him to disrupt the newspaper business in two ways. First, he lowered the price of a paper to one penny, a price that just about everyone could afford. Second, he scoured the prisons, police departments, and tenements to find the most salacious and eye-grabbing headlines available. The rationale behind these changes was devilishly insightful. Day understood that, if he could amass a large enough audience, i.e. get enough attention, he could then sell advertisements to businesses, which would supply his profits. Suddenly, an unexpected revolution had occurred. A new product was available for purchase – the attention of you and me, ordinary men and women.

All of this would be just a tidbit of interesting history if it did not touch upon a further fact. Up until the nineteenth century there had only been one institution in the history of the world that was interested in captivating the attention of ordinary people, *the church*. Businesses didn't care about attention; they wanted profit. Governments didn't value attention; they valued tax revenue and loyalty. The church coveted the attention of ordinary people because the church understood the power of an ancient spiritual

---

13. Tim Wu, *The Attention Merchants: the Epic Scramble to Get inside Our Heads* (New York: Random House, 2016).

discipline, practicing the presence of God. Christians had long learned that the only way to become like God was to maintain an awareness of God.[14]

Gone are the Arcadian days when Adam and Eve walked through the garden without billboards and click-bait to distract them. We now live in a setting in which no commodity is prized more than the mental awareness of an average Joe. Media, technology, and advertising is more familiar to us than is the sight of trees, the sound of birds, or the feel of dirt. Our ecosystem is a technological world.[15] Companies purchase dibs to our attention and invest millions developing strategies to captivate us. And the strategies work. Consider how the cumulative advent of radio, network TV, cable, the internet, cell phones, social media, and the smart phone has changed the way in which normal human beings experience the world. Companies can now access our minds at any moment of any day. And we gratefully allow them to do so.

Although there is nothing new under the sun, we must recognize that the chief front of spiritual combat is different in different eras. Christians have never found the disciplines of prayer or meditation easy to perform. They have always found ways of being distracted even if the distraction was limited to telling yarns by the fire. Nevertheless, at least in the past there were not so many ways to

---

14.   In the early nineteenth century Georg Hegel observed that reading the newspaper was replacing morning prayer. Two hundred years ago this insight was new and shocking. Today checking one's phone before opening a Bible is taken for granted.

15.   The classic treatment of this new technological environment is Jacques Ellul, *The Technological Society* (New York: Vintage Books, 1964). See also Neil Postman, *Technopoly* (New York: Vintage Books, 1993). Postman is a much easier read than Ellul.

be distracted or such advanced technology being used to captivate attention. A world without radio, TV, internet, or iPhones is a world far more conducive to meditation. Focusing on God becomes even more difficult than before when a moment-by-moment Instagram feed meows in the background like an unfed cat.

We need to connect all of this back to our central topic regarding men. Men are struggling, in part, because they live in a hostile environment that increases the difficulty of performing basic spiritual activities. Spiritual growth depends upon abiding in Christ (John 15:7), being transformed in mind (Rom. 12:2), sober-mindedness (1 Pet. 1:13), and meditating on the Word (Ps. 1, 119). Without a tight rein on our attention, the basest of appetites are fanned into flames while the embers of divine love are snuffed out. If it is true that the highest capacity of the human person is to abide in the knowledge and love of God (John 17:3), then secular companies are correct: there is no resource of greater value than the attention of ordinary men and women. The spare moments of our attention are not loose pennies but nuggets of gold. We ought to remember that for the Aztecs gold was considered to be 'the excrement of the gods', and they happily gave the conquistadors as much gold as the Spaniards desired. What was the consequence of such foolishness? Ruin and slavery. The very resource that could have given the Aztecs leverage over their opponent became a spur to their demise.

Men ought to learn a lesson from this. The gate of our attention leads to the treasury of our heart. Among the many reasons why men are spiritually stuck is the fact that many underestimate the value of their attention.

The Depth

◁◁◁◆◆◆▷▷▷

Growing up my grandparents had a swimming pool. Along the floor of this pool there was a gradual slope that led to a sudden drop. Although there was no external indicator, I remember as a kid knowing very clearly when I entered 'the deep end'. You could feel the difference.

We are now entering the deeper side of the problem of why men are not growing. To admit this does not detract from the seriousness of any of the factors that have been explored thus far. All of the aspects of the problem are significant and merit careful thought. However, some aspects are more important than others, and the last two touch upon the most fundamental part of the human person, what the Bible labels *the heart*. If, to a degree at least, the earlier sections indicated that the primary cause of the struggle of men was external, the perspective now needs to shift. The objective moving forward is to perform open heart surgery in order to see how the ancient problem of sin manifests itself among contemporary men.

Men are Dis-Attracted

There is nothing more fundamental to human life than *love*. By 'love' I mean neither the heavenly love that the Holy Spirit supplies, nor the romantic love that Romeo felt for Juliet, nor the affection that a young boy has for a puppy. I am talking about the kind of love that Saint Augustine describes as being an invisible force directing all of human action. In the *Confession* Augustine famously says, 'My love is my weight, and wherever I am carried, it is this weight that carries me.' Anticipating more recent discoveries regarding human psychology, Augustine understood that it was not the calculating intellect or the imperious will that sat on the throne of the human heart. Love reigned. My delight is my desire, and my desire is the chief executive casting the final vote.

It is worth probing a little further in order to understand clearly the degree to which love governs the mundane behavior of men. Unbeknownst to most guys, every human being is born with an internal navigation system which is incessantly calculating a route through life toward a fixed destination. The first action this navigation system performs is to determine an object of ultimate worth.[16] This usually happens unconsciously. A child is born into a white, Western, middle-class family. He is surrounded with emblems of hard work, discipline, and achievement. No one needs to preach the gospel of success to him. He inhales the value as he is ushered between private music lessons, gifted reading programs, and select sports teams. By the time this boy is a teenager he has partaken of enough public rituals to be a full devotee of the religion my-worth-is-determined-by-achievement. His navigation system is now programed with a precise destination. The object he desires

---

16. An in-depth treatment of this 'navigation system' can be found in Charles Taylor, *Sources of the Self: the Making of the Modern Identity* (Cambridge: Harvard University Press, 1989), pp. 3-24.

as if it were life itself is success. The threat he fears as if it were death itself is *failure*, the absence of success.[17]

Now once this navigation system has a fixed destination, step two occurs: love calculates and re-calculates a route from *where I am* to *where I need to be*. This route-planning is an ongoing work that never ceases. The heart is always prompting us down a strategic course, like a kind of spiritual Google Map indicating 'turn left', 'reverse and go back', or 'you have arrived at your destination'. This is why, whenever we are faced with a significant decision, the most important factor is not deliberation, or will-power, but *perception*.[18] The key question that prompts us down the path of life is this: which option on the table brings me closer to—or enables me to enjoy more of—my chief object of delight? If I live for success, I will consistently make choices that promote success. The same could be said of holiness, fitness, wealth, pleasure, comfort, family, or power.

This background is necessary in order to understand the spiritual struggles of men. I am convinced that one of the most significant reasons why Christian men neglect spiritual growth is because, deep down, their hearts are disordered (i.e. out of order).[19]

---

17. One could substitute for 'success' beauty, comfort, knowledge, culture, fun, power, pleasure, fitness, holiness or any number of other things.

18. David Brooks has a user friendly description of perception in *The Social Animal: the Hidden Sources of Love, Character, and Achievement* (New York: Random House, 2011). The more philosophically minded will find a thorough analysis of such moral vision in Iris Murdoch's book *Existentialists and Mystics: Writings on Philosophy and Literature* (New York: Penguin Books, 1999), pp. 299-362.

19. David Brooks discusses disordered love in *The Road to Character* (New York: Random House, 2015), chapter 8. See also Etienne Gilson, *The Christian Philosophy of Saint Augustine* (New York: Random House, 1960), pp. 135-140.

Lesser goods are valued higher than greater goods. The problem is not that men don't love God or that men don't value spiritual maturity. The problem is that they love minor goods more than the Greatest Good and that they value little things above the Chief Thing. At the end of the day, love always wins. Whatever a man loves most will direct the course of his life. If a man loves wrongly, he will live wrongly. Willpower, at best, is a levee that can only hold back the floodwaters of love for a finite period of time. Once love achieves a certain volume, nothing but grace can constrain it.

More than once I have confessed that I used to think that men struggled because they were apathetic. I now believe the deep problem affecting men is not apathy, or indolence, but idolatry. The vast majority of men are passionate creatures. The problem is not a lack of religious zeal; the problem is that their zeal is directed toward the wrong religion.

Men need to feel the sharp edge of this truth. Unless their consciences are pricked, there will be no self-understanding, and without true self-knowledge there will be no change. For this reason, like a prosecuting attorney, I want to compile the evidence so that men understand the degree to which all of us are guilty of misdirected love.

1 – The Evidence of Time

If a man wants to know what he incontestably values, all he has to do is log his time use over a week and review the data. Time is a non-renewable resource, like coal, not water. For this reason, people don't waste time; they invest time. They spend their time according to what they value. Stare long enough at a spreadsheet logging daily consumption of minutes and hours and a scale of priorities jumps into view like a skeleton through an X-ray. The bones of career, fun, friendship, health, faith, etc. come together in a visible structure, the order being determined by a simple fact: the degree to which I cannot *not* have something.

Thus, for example, most men cannot not have a profound and detailed knowledge of College Football. They need to know the key players of important teams, understand the different divisions, have a functional knowledge of strategic formations on offense and defense, see game-changing plays, and be able to talk intelligently about the history of the game. They are passionate about football, so much so that they invest more time and energy in football than they do in Bible study, prayer, or deeds of mercy. Fast-forward through life and this explains why so many Christian men have a preschool knowledge of God but a post-doc in armchair quarterbacking. What is the problem? Too many men are content to live without a deep knowledge of God. The same is not true of football. The proof is in the time-sheet: they love football more than they love God.

2 – The Evidence of Anxiety

Another way of measuring care is strategic worry, also known as care or productive anxiety. People who study the brain contrast system 1 and system 2 thinking.[20] On the one hand, system 1 is fast, instinctive and emotional. It requires as much effort as craving a donut. System 2, on the other, is slow, deliberate, and rational. Directing system 2 is exhaustive work, like convincing yourself at mile twenty-four of a marathon not to stop because achievement is

---

20. The distinction is found in Daniel Kahneman, *Thinking, Fast and Slow* (New York: Farrar, Straus, and Giroux, 2011).

better than rest. Now if a man wants to discover what he really cares about, all he needs to do is answer the following questions: what do I consistently think about? Where do I invest my worry? What grips my mind when I cannot sleep and the clock strikes 1 a.m.? What do I strategically pursue with all of my mental resources? Christian men must be aware that, where the mind is, there the heart is also. Thinking is too vital a resource for this not to be the case.

So, then, what do most guys fixate on? Career. Sex. Health. Physique. Adventure. Fun. There are not a lot of guys in the modern world sitting in cubicles coveting the scriptural imagination of C. S. Lewis. Rare is the man in the gym dreaming about strategic ways to reach his neighbors with the gospel. For every man in the church intentionally seeking the prayer life of George Mueller there are scores, if not hundreds, concerned more about building a 'man-cave' or perfecting the barbeque than radically re-thinking their prayer lives. Why is this? The truth is not hard to find: the priorities of God are not the priorities of men. Action follows love like a dog its master.

3 – The Evidence of Sacrifice

A third metric for measuring love is sacrifice, the test of what I am willing to give up in order to have something better. Most of what Christian men pursue today is not intrinsically evil. Career is not evil. Neither is fitness, nor family, nor laughing among friends, nor resting from work. However, one of the challenges of life is bumping up against our finitude. There are not enough hours of the day, or years in a lifetime, to enjoy, experience, and do everything. Therefore, choices must be made. Lesser goods must often be relinquished, not because they are bad, but because higher ends must be fulfilled.

One indicator of love is my willingness to sacrifice objects of lesser worth in order to draw nearer to what I supremely value. Am I willing, for example, to reject a promotion in order to protect time and mental freedom for prayer? Am I willing to have a couple of extra inches around my waistline in order to be a better father, husband, and church member? Am I willing to miss a round of golf in order to visit a neighbor in the hospital? These are not insignificant questions. What I care about reveals itself in the daily choices that I make. If I consistently sacrifice my obedience to Christ for competing objectives, the evidence is all but irrefutable: regardless of what I say in public, or feel in private, the truth is I don't care about spiritual maturity, at least not as much as I care about other things. Make no mistake – love is not a feeling; love is a motive for action. If action is consistently stillborn, a dearth of love is the problem. This is the principle behind Jesus' statement, 'He who loves me, keeps my commandments' (John 14:21).[21]

Men, the evidence is plain. Why are we spiritually stagnant? My conviction is that feeding the branches of exhaustion, frustration, loneliness, and distraction is an idolatrous heart that values pennies more than dollars. The old Proverb needs to be pondered anew: 'Keep your heart with all vigilance, for from it flows the springs of life' (4:23).

Men are Unconvinced

Where I currently live there are a lot of pier and beam foundations. The concept behind this type of foundation is simple even if the

---

21. Ceil Alexander captures this truth in the following lines of a hymn: 'Jesus calls us from the worship/Of the vain world's golden store,/From each idol that would keep us,/Saying: Christian love me more.'

engineering can be complex. Basically, there are several piers that support the flooring of a house. These piers are carefully grounded to ensure that the floors, walls, and roof of the house are secure and able to withstand both the weight of the overall structure as well as the wear of time and weather. Now imagine that Dennis the Menace moves into my neighborhood and decides that he wants to play a prank on Mr Wilson. Dennis decides to shimmy into the crawl space under Mr Wilson's house and to knock out a few of the piers holding up the building. If Dennis succeeds and keeps doing this, one after another, what would happen? The house would begin to cave in. If enough were removed, the house would crumble.

This is a useful picture for thinking about how theological convictions support spiritual growth. Human beings are not pure-bred rational animals. We do not always act in accordance with what we believe. However, human beings are reason-dependent animals. If we lack belief, we are all but guaranteed not to behave in particular ways. What is the relevance of this? I am convinced that one final reason why Christian men are struggling is because key convictions are absent from their intellectual framework.[22] Christian men are, in other words, like houses built on damaged foundations. The walls and ceilings of godliness are collapsing because the belief system supporting godliness is inadequate.

I do not have the space here to attempt to outline all of the convictions that are useful for supporting discipleship. But, fortunately, I do not need to do this. When piers are damaged, the task

---

22. For understanding the role of an intellectual framework in shaping the identity of a person see Charles Taylor, *A Secular Age* (Cambridge: Harvard University Press, 2007), pp. 1-25.

at hand is not surveying the piers in good condition, but finding the piers requiring repair. Such is my goal here. My work with men has indicated that, among evangelical believers, a lot of important doctrines are in decent working order. Yet others, of vital significance, are strangely missing. It is the missing, or damaged, beliefs of contemporary Christian men that need special treatment.

1 – Growth Requires Effort

In the last twenty-five years there has been a remarkable recovery of the truths of grace. However, too often, these doctrines have been communicated carelessly, leaving guys confused, even deceived. For many guys, grace has become a license for immaturity. How has this happened?

First, careless preaching of grace has made some guys content to cohabit with sin. They reach this mindset via the following logic: if God loves me in spite of my sin, and if Jesus has clothed me with His righteousness, then sin really isn't that big of a deal. Sin is more like a blunder, like childishness, than a threat, like a virus. A further belief entrenches this mindset even further – the inevitability of sin. Since sin is always going to be in my heart, in one form or another, what difference does it make if I stamp out one weed only to see another replace it? Jesus will clean up the problem after I die.

Now I need to be clear what I am saying. My point is not that Christian men today are entirely tolerant of sin. Most Christians are trying in earnest to resist or uproot various sins in their lives. The point is this: a kind of despair, a degree of fatalism, or a hint of permissiveness keeps men from hoping and attempting radical self-transformation in and through the Holy Spirit. Few are the men today who feel the hope or urgency required to storm the strongholds of sin under the banner of 2 Corinthians 7:1: 'Therefore, having these promises, beloved, let us cleanse ourselves of all filthiness of the flesh and spirit, perfecting holiness in the fear of God' (KJV). For too many, grace is an excuse for doling out permanent resident cards to at least a few pet vices.

Yet, to think this way is to abuse grace. Grace is not a motive for an indulgent attitude of self-acceptance. Grace is the liberating declaration that I am no longer defined by my sin or held captive by its power. Because of grace I can hope, I can fight – I can have a holy discontentment with the state of my heart believing that, with the help of Almighty God, change is possible. Yes, perfection, like the clouds above me, will elude my grasp. Yet, any despair resulting from my imperfection is a sign that I have not really understood the message of grace. Grace is the strength and incentive to aim for the stars even if my progress will be measured in inches.

This leads us into a second way that grace has been wrongly applied to spirituality. I continually meet Christians today who mistake effort for legalism. They think that any strenuous attempt to improve one's character is not only self-defeating but an insult to the grace of God. The underlying belief is that growing in righteousness, 'sanctification', is primarily a passive action, something that God does for us without requiring much sweat from our brow. But in thinking this way Christians mistake God's method of justification for His method of sanctification. For justification, the Christian does nothing more than receive by faith the free gift of salvation. However, for sanctification, while no less dependent on the grace of God, we are much more involved in the process. J. I. Packer highlights this point writing, 'By the Spirit's enabling, Christians resolve to do particular things that are right, and actually do them, and thus form habits of doing right things, and out of these habits comes a character that is right.' He later adds, 'Holiness teaching that skips over disciplined persistence in the well-doing that forms holy habits is thus weak; habit forming is the Spirit's ordinary way of leading us on in holiness.'[23] The point we need to glean from Packer is this: any application of grace that relieves Christians of the need to exert themselves strenuously for the sake of holiness is an abuse of grace. The message of grace does not eliminate effort from the Christian life. On the contrary, the message of grace gives us hope that—due to the power of the Holy Spirit—the effort of a child (and at most we are children) is not in vain.

2 – Christians Will be Judged

Thomas Jefferson is famous for having produced a version of the New Testament with all of the supernatural edited out. I sometimes wonder if a revised edition is in circulation today, not with the miracles removed, but rather all of the Biblical references to individual judgment.[24] I have repeatedly found throughout my ministry that a lot of good Christian men—evangelicals especially—either don't believe in a personal judgment or are so confused by the thought (how it harmonizes with grace) that they live in blithe denial.

The confusion is due, in part, to Christians mistaking condemnation and accountability. On the one hand, Paul is clear that there is no condemnation for anyone in Christ Jesus. In saying this, Paul

---

23. J. I. Packer, *Keep in Step with the Spirit* (Old Tappan: Fleming H. Revell, 1984), pp. 108-9.

24. A few passages to reflect upon are 2 Corinthians 5:10; Romans 14:7-12; 1 Corinthians 3:10-15; Colossians 3:22-25; 1 Peter 4:5; Hebrews 9:27; and 1 Corinthians 4:5.

eliminates the worry that a Christian will be put to final shame, that there could be a final cut after which some believing Christians don't make the team. Paul alleviates our worry by stating in plain terms that everyone who professes Christ will be saved (Rom. 5:8-9, 10:9). On the other hand, Paul is equally clear that freedom from condemnation is not freedom from accountability. Each individual, Christians included, will be judged by Christ for the things done in the body. In connection with this, rewards will be given (or missed) based on personal obedience. Now there are a lot of profound questions to be asked about the nature of such rewards. Much is unclear. What is undeniable, however, is that all Christians ought to live each day in view of a final review.[25]

The relevant point for us to consider is how inattentiveness to final judgment affects the spiritual maturity of contemporary men. Most importantly, ignorance of final judgment convinces guys that they can't waste their lives. If ultimately all Christians receive the same inheritance, and if this life has no bearing on the life to come (other than determining who gets to 'heaven'), the logical conclusion is that my present life has little or no eternal significance. Abiding in this logic, a lot of Christian men feel little urgency to redeem the time.[26]

---

25. Modern praise and worship have reinforced this forgetfulness. Most of the songs sung in churches today speak of Christians being translated into final glory with the seamlessness of a Lady Gaga costume change. Only a handful make any reference to final judgment. The result is a lop-sided spirituality whereby Christians affirm one New Testament doctrine (immediate entry into heaven) while blanking another (individual judgment). For an example of a classic hymn that focuses attention on Christ as judge, see Charles Wesley's 'Thou Judge of Quick and Dead'.

26. Men need to reflect on Spurgeon's advice to one of his sons: 'Time flies and the opportunity of doing good flies with it. However diligent you may

Although they would agree, for example, that deeds of mercy and service are a better use of time than watching sports or lifting weights, they do not worry about justifying their timesheet before the bar of Christ. The general assumption is that all foolishness will be forgotten on the other side of the grave.

But this mentality does not square with the teaching of the apostles. Paul, in particular, warns us that each life is contributing something to the work of God. The contribution of some is of the value of gold, silver, and jewels; the contribution of others, wood, hay, and straw. The rest of Paul's teaching on this point is best communicated in his own words:

> Each one's work will become manifest, for the Day will disclose it, because it will be revealed by fire, and the fire will test what sort of work each one has done. If the work that anyone has built on the foundation survives, he will receive a reward. If anyone's work is burned up, he will suffer loss, though he himself will be saved, but only as through fire (1 Cor. 3:13-15).

For us, the application of these verses is that men ought to think twice before handing over every spare moment to Netflix. Salvation by grace does not eliminate personal accountability. Even if I cannot lose my salvation (Paul emphasizes this point saying, 'he himself will be saved'), I can bury some of my talents. I fear that some men are too easily content with their spiritual development because, deep down, they don't believe that the present moment has ultimate significance.

---

be in the future, you can only do the work of 1875 in 1875, and if you leave it undone now, it will be undone unto all eternity.' The same can be said of the present year.

3 – The World is a Battlefield

Fifty years ago Tozer wrote, 'The idea that this world is a playground instead of a battleground has now been accepted in practice by the vast majority of Christians.' The statement is truer today than when the ink first dried. Civilization and culture have united to convince men that the greatest evil in life is *missing out*. On the one hand, civilization has—for us in the West—removed the grievances of the premodern world. On a typical Saturday, severe illness, famine, and war feel no more of a threat than iron chariots and longbows. On the other, pop culture repeatedly tells us that the highest aims of life are experiencing thrills, making memories, and having fun. Put ingredient one and ingredient two together and the world does not *feel* like a dangerous warzone, as depicted in the New Testament, but like a trip to Disney World. And every child knows that there are only three rules at Disney: have fun, be safe, and respect others.

A host of problems emerge from this illusion. First, with civilization keeping us safe and prosperous, and pop culture directing our passions and lifestyle, the need for 'god' (regardless of who you think he is) is reduced to that of a therapist and a life insurance policy. All we need from religion is something to boost our spirits when depressed and something to unlock the pearly gates after we die. Otherwise, 'god' does not factor into the life plan.

But, second, this playground mentality eliminates the need for earnest spiritual training. Rare is the child who prepares himself for the playground. Little boys do not do pull-ups in order to improve on the monkey bars. Little girls do not enroll in CrossFit to go faster on the Merry-Go-Round. The idea of rigorously training for the playground is every bit as ridiculous as the thought of getting a good night's sleep before eating Chinese food. The goal of the playground is not to perform well, but to maximize fun before time runs out – before the teacher whistles or dad says, 'let's go!'

The application of this ought to be clear. The more men succumb to the illusion that life is a quest for fun, the less they need God, and the more apathetic they are regarding temptation. The words of Peter begin to sound a little extreme, even paranoid: 'Beloved, I urge you as sojourners and exiles to abstain from the passions of the flesh, which wage war against your soul' (1 Pet. 2:11). Like the disciples in Gethsemane, men begin to sleep when they are supposed to be keeping watch. They forget about the prowling lion who is ready to pounce in the bush. This, I fear, is the condition of many Christian men.

4 – One Thing is Needed

The busyness of modern life needs no further description. Society, culture, class, parents, employers, government, marriage, children, church, and self all have a different set of expectations that add weight to the burden of life. Men feel immense pressure to attempt to mimic the Greek titan Atlas whose job it was to shoulder the weight of the sky. Of course, men cannot do it. They are mortals, not gods, and the result of their pride is a range of painful injuries including addiction, burnout, anxiety, depression, anger, shame, and angst.

Recently, I was asked what verse Christian men need to hear more than any other. My answer was Luke 10:42, 'One thing is needed.' Repeatedly, Jesus' perspective on life is scandalously simple. There is no bucket-list. There is no call for rabid multitasking. There is *one thing*. In fact, Jesus promises that if our chief objective is earnestly pursued then God will supply our other needs. In the Sermon on the Mount, He says, 'Therefore do not be anxious, saying, "What shall we eat?" or "What shall we drink?" or "What shall we wear?"… But seek first the kingdom of God and his righteousness and all these things will be added to you' (Matt. 6:31, 33). Christian discipleship might be challenging, but it is not complicated. The objectives of life are reduced to a bare minimum, one.[27] Our calling is to follow Christ.

The same simplicity evident in the life and teaching of Jesus is evident in the life and teaching of Paul. Paul may have had a difficult life, an adventurous life, and an energetic life, but he did not have a complicated life. For this reason he was able to write to the Philippians, 'One thing I do' (Phil. 3:13). Paul's tasks were wide, but his focus was narrow. He did not attempt to do everything. He did not attempt to experience everything. His agenda was to finish the race God had given *him* to run.

Spiritual growth will forever suffer among men until they are convinced of their need to simplify.[28] To attempt everything is to accomplish nothing. In fact, even Jesus did not attempt to do more than the Father had asked of Him. In His high priestly prayer, He confessed that there were limitations on His calling. 'I have brought you glory on earth by finishing the work you gave

---

27.   The great Czech reformer John Amos Commenius wrote a treatise on this truth called *The One Thing Needed*. An English translation can be found online: http://moravianarchives.org/images/pdfs/Unum%20Necessarium.pdf

28.   Interestingly, secular wisdom corresponds to spiritual wisdom on this point. For example, Warren Buffet recommends that ambitious entrepreneurs write a list of their top 25 goals in life, number them in sequence, tear off numbers 6-25, throw these into the trash, and once this is done, focus exclusively on 1-5. Even secular business leaders appreciate that a fierce commitment to simplicity is a prerequisite to any form of success.

me to do' (John 17:4 NIV). Jesus did not do everything. He limited Himself to the work God had given Him to accomplish. Men today are dangerously naive if they believe that they can do more than Jesus, the Son of God, did. In fact, they are worse than naive. They are proud, and pride only ever leads to one thing, *a fall* (Prov. 16:18).

5 – The Spiritual Potential of Ordinary Men

A lot of men think that the heroes of faith are a superior class of human beings, like Lebron James or Ronaldo, freaks among mortals. They think it preposterous that God would take the weak things of this world—the Gideons, Jeremiahs, and Peters—and use them as select instruments. They have never dared to hope that the oft-quoted words of D. L. Moody might apply to them: 'The world has yet to see what God can do with a man fully yielded to Him.' Without spiritual hope, a lot of men are without spiritual ambition, unwilling to prepare for what God might do through them because they already know the answer, *not much*.[29]

The result of such despair is often buried talents and missed opportunities. A man may wrongly conclude that, because God has not called him to a foreign mission field, he does not need to train, like Hudson Taylor, in courageous faith. Likewise, he might think that, because he is not Dawson Trotman, the founder of the Navigators, he does not need to pursue a rigorous Scripture memory program.

---

29. Men need to capture their ambition and use it for spiritual pursuits. J. Oswald Sanders reminds us, 'Desiring to excel is not a sin. It is motivation that determines ambition's character. Our Lord never taught against the urge to high achievement. He did expose and condemn unworthy motivation. All Christians are called to develop God-given talents, to make the most of their lives, and to develop to the fullest their God-given gifts and capabilities.' J. Oswald Sanders, *Spiritual Leadership* (Chicago, Moody Publishers, 2007).

Bedazzled by the glamor of famous Christians, a man might resign to be a benchwarmer since God has not called him to 'fulltime ministry'. But to think this way is to overlook the spiritual potential of an ordinary life. Regardless of church development through the centuries, the vision of the New Testament is one whereby regular men and women extend the mission of God through their everyday lives. There are not two categories of Christians, saints and laymen. In the kingdom of God, everyone is on active duty, and everyone shares in the same exciting calling to go unto all nations and to make disciples.

Nothing is more pernicious to Christianity than drawing a strict line between the sacred and the secular, thinking that fulltime workers, for example, are ordained clergy and everyone else is a volunteer. Such an attitude depletes spiritual drive and convinces men that there is nothing significant within the kingdom for them to do. Peter Drucker once said that burnout is usually a copout for being bored. There is spiritual application in this statement. If men do not believe they are needed, they will struggle to find motivation. Every Christian man ought to think and act as if the frontline of the war between heaven and hell crossed through the middle of his home.

Further missing 'piers' could be discovered that are absent from the theological frameworks of men. However, the chief point has been made. The structural damage evident in the discipleship of men has deep and underlying sources. Slothfulness and obsessive busyness are the result of core truths being misunderstood or never heard at all. This creates long-term problems as men seek to maintain a stable Christian identity in a dark and confusing world. Without a sure foundation, no house can stand (Matt. 7:24-27).

Final Diagnosis

Why are men failing to achieve their potential in Christ? As mentioned at the outset the problem is complicated. There are surface behavioral factors, like an attention economy and a cult of busyness, mixing with deep spiritual factors, like disbelief and disordered love, creating a toxic environment for spiritual growth. The accusation that men are lazy or apathetic is unjust. A lot of Christian men are highly productive, self-motivated workers. They are passionate and pour themselves fervently into a lot of different endeavors. They are committed and shoulder heavy burdens in multiple fields of responsibility, including society, church, the workplace, and at home. What, then, is the problem? The problem is a little bit of everything: men are exhausted, frustrated, alone, distracted, nearsighted, ill-informed, and idolatrous. When facing the problem of why men are stuck, the diagnosis is complicated, which means one thing for us as we move forward: if the diagnosis has multiple parts, the remedy will too. There is no pill that can quickly be swallowed in order to improve the condition of men. There are no shortcuts to expedite the process. Jesus was speaking directly to us when He said,

'Whoever does not bear his own cross and come after me cannot be my disciple. For which of you, desiring to build a tower, does not first sit down and count the cost, whether he has enough to complete it? Otherwise, when he has laid a foundation and is not able to finish, all who see it begin to mock him, saying, 'This man began to build and was not able to finish' (Luke 14:27-30).

PART 2

The Solution

◁◁◁◆◆◆▷▷▷

The Baseline Candidate

The summer after my freshman year of college I went to Officer Candidate School for the Marine Corps. At the time, fresh after the horrors of 9/11, I was contemplating joining the armed forces. Officer Candidate School provided a way of sticking a foot in the water without having to sign away multiple years of life. I will never forget my first afternoon at Quantico. Hundreds of young men had been recruited, left nervous parents waving at airports, and made the cross-country trip to Virginia. We arrived in buses and were taken into an auditorium to wait in silence for chaos to erupt.

The training kick-started as you might expect. Like a bomb detonating, drill instructors ripped doors open, threw tables over, and shoved guys toward the exits of the building. Before any of us had a clue what was happening, we were dressed in PT garb and cycling through a set of fitness drills in order to see who could stay and who could not. My memory is that almost a third of the recruits were cut on day one of OCS. I'll never forget the image of seeing a young man hanging on a pull-up bar, weeping, because he could not meet the minimum standard of an officer candidate.

The thought that still strikes me as I recall the image is this: how did it happen that so many young men were totally unprepared for Marine training? How did they not realize what they were committing to? While I did not have as much assistance preparing for the boot camp as I would have liked, I did have two recruiters who at least made sure that I knew the minimum fitness standards to endure the summer. Evidently, a lot of young men did not even have this. Whether due to self-confidence, naivety, or deception, they had committed to something they were unable to finish. The results were heartbreaking to watch.

Here is the point of the illustration: my goal in this section is to describe what I call a 'baseline candidate'. Before any young man stepped onto a plane to travel to Quantico, he should have had someone in his life advising him regarding the minimum fitness required (here I am thinking of fitness as a broader category than physical strength – mental fitness, basic skills, etc.) to complete the summer training. Of course, entering into OCS with such fitness would not have guaranteed that any individual candidate would in fact finish. However, such fitness was a basic condition without which a recruit was all but guaranteed to fail.

I believe that Christian men need something similar to a model of a baseline candidate, even if the analogy to OCS is imperfect. Where the analogy fails is the degree to which it suggests that we as Christians must in some way get our act together before the process of spiritual maturity can occur. The difference between training in godliness and training as an Officer Candidate must be stated clearly. Maturing Christians are not a spiritual elite who are enabled to grow because they are the cream of the crop. Every Christian is equally dependent upon grace and the power of the Holy Spirit. Only by grace does any man find strength to grow.

Nonetheless, there is truth communicated in the idea of being prepared as a candidate for maturity. Jesus does, after all, tell His disciples that they must 'count the cost' (Luke 14:28) if they want to follow Him. Personally, I am convinced that there are a lot of men in the church who have never done the math. To use Bonhoeffer's oft-quoted phrase, they have accepted a 'cheap grace' and are therefore surprised by the difficulties of bearing a cross. This section will be a success if it does nothing more than eliminate *naivety* among Christian men. What follows is not a self-righteous attempt to describe an inner circle of Christians, but a loving warning that men ought to show no less seriousness when preparing for discipleship than they would show if signing up for Marine boot camp.

The guiding question for this section is this: 'What are the basic conditions that promote spiritual growth among men?' Promote is the keyword here. Let me be clear – these conditions do not guarantee growth; neither does their absence necessarily mean that a man will not grow. Growth is in God's hands, not ours. And yet divine sovereignty does not eliminate human responsibility. Therefore, even while depending on God's mercy, a man is negligent if he does not also ask the question, 'What can I do to prepare?' This section aims at providing a portrait of preparedness.

There is one further application to make from the image of Officer Candidate School. The goal of OCS was not to graduate *officers* but to send *candidates* down a path that, if followed, would lead them on to becoming commissioned as officers in the Marine Corps. For good reason I have been speaking of candidates instead of graduates. The purpose of this book is to help men to begin *to begin* the process of spiritual development. Therefore, the silhouette that will be traced in this section will not be the figure of a perfect man, a man at the end of his journey, but rather the outline of a man who is packed and ready for the start of a much longer process.

Five aspects of a baseline candidate will be discussed: captivation, clarity, competence, camaraderie, and self-control. This list of traits is a product of thinking about the relationship between two factors: (1) the consistent problems that limit spiritual growth among men and (2) the consistent traits that are evident in maturing men of faith. Could more be stated regarding the internal makeup of a man who is prepared for serious discipleship? Certainly. Yet, keep in mind that our goal is relevance, not comprehensiveness. *What are the qualities that best prepare a man to mature in Christ?* This question is the trail we will follow.

Men Need Captivation

◁◁◁◆◆◆▷▷▷

In ancient warfare there were two ways for a walled city to face an oncoming army. One way was to bolt the gate, store as much food as possible, and to prepare for either a direct assault or an extended siege. The other way was to throw open the gates, change the flag, and to welcome a foreign king with oaths of loyalty and showers of confetti. Spiritually, captivation is what happens when we throw down the arms of the heart and eagerly recognize a new object of devotion as sovereign in our life. I remember my first experience of this. I was a child and was watching Michael Jordan play basketball. I could hear the crowd; I could see the beauty; I could taste the glory. Suddenly, my allegiance shifted. I am not sure what existed as the center of my gravity before that moment, but in a flash one sun had been replaced by another. I identified with a new 'god' although I would not have labeled it such. Basketball along with its chief prophet, Michael Jordan, was my religion. I was a devotee to the cult. I was captivated.

Defining Captivation

Captivation is the word that I use for a heart that has been fiercely gripped by a vision of unparalleled beauty and goodness.[1] From

---

1. The idea of captivation is rendered beautifully in the hymn 'Hast Thou Heard Him, Seen Him, Known Him?' by Ora Rowan. The chorus reads, 'Captivated

what I can perceive, not every person experiences captivation. A lot of people are content to navigate life using a constellation of smallish goods like career, fun, family, health, hobbies, and spirituality. These goods are like stars in the night sky. Some shine brighter than others, but none shines so brightly that, like the sun, it overpowers the rest with its blinding light. You know when you meet a person who has not experienced captivation because their goal for living is a 'balanced life'. Like a candelabra, the ideal is for each good to sparkle appropriately. Something is wrong if one flashes so brightly that it detracts due attention from the others.

In contrast, the first sign of captivation is an imbalanced life. You know a person who is captivated because one ultimate object towers like the sun over the earth such that nothing else can be seen except in its light. Other things have worth only insofar as they reflect, or refract, or make present, the highest good. Ultimately, there is only one light; everything else, at best, is a mirror.

Now it is worth stating that there is nothing peculiarly religious about the objects that can captivate the hearts of men. Any number of ordinary things can seize the deepest love of a man and proclaim itself a 'god'. Success, knowledge, power, beauty, fitness, culture, popularity, wealth, pleasure, sports cars, golf, and fishing – the candidates are as numerous as the passions of men. What makes captivation religious is not the object worshiped but the worshipful devotion directed to an object. Captivation occurs when a man decides to be a monotheist instead of a polytheist. When he clears the pantheon of the heart so that there is a single altar, then, and only then, is he captivated.

---

by his beauty/Worthy tribute haste to bring;/Let his peerless worth constrain thee/Crown him now unrivaled king.'

The point I want to extract from this is the following: I am convinced that no man will make serious progress toward spiritual maturity until he is captivated by the glory of Christ. To attempt discipleship without captivation is like entering into a marriage without a deep desire to have and to hold a single woman. Any man who goes into his wedding day with a heart divided between three or four girlfriends will be a failure as a husband. The struggle will be no less for a Christian who reduces Christ to something smaller than the sum of all wisdom, goodness, beauty, honor, truth, and pleasure. There is only one face that perfectly reveals the hidden glory of God. That face is Jesus. There is only one door that makes divine life accessible to us. That door is Jesus. Understanding this—no, *experiencing this*— is fundamental to continued growth as a Christian.

Why Men Need Captivation

There are three reasons why captivation is of such importance for discipleship. The first is that captivation has a unique ability to unseat the idols of the heart.[2] We have discussed already the way in which men are not only distracted, but dis-*attracted*. More than apathy, we have seen that idolatry is the problem handicapping the growth of men. Through a variety of subtle tactics Christian men are duped into over-estimating the value of finite goods. We are like bidders at an auction who get caught up in the proceedings and end up paying more for objects than they are worth. Thus,

---

2. The great spiritual writer Walter Hilton notes, 'Love slays sin.' A rich psychology of how this happens is found in his book *Toward a Perfect Love: the Spiritual Counsel of Walter Hilton,* trans. David L. Jeffrey (Vancouver: Regent College Publishing, 1985), pp. 71-94. See also Thomas Chalmer's invaluable sermon, 'The Expulsive Power of a New Affection' which is available online.

for example, a career becomes more than a paycheck and a way to serve Christ. A career becomes the bedrock of an identity, the only trustworthy path to self-fulfillment. Sex, or exercise, or comfort, transforms from a limited pleasure to an unquenchable appetite. A little thing becomes the only thing, and men soon find themselves shackled by the chains of their own deep emotions. The problem is not outside of us; the problem is inside of us. This is what makes idolatry so difficult. Having opened wide the gates of the heart, we wake up to the realization that a counterfeit is on the throne, but that we have forfeited the very power that might have resisted him, *our love.*

Being captivated by the glory of Christ is the secret to mounting a coup against a false god. A lot of men may remember the difficulty they felt trying to break up with a toxic girlfriend. The most efficient method of getting over a bad girlfriend is to meet a fantastic girl. Being gripped by something better is always the easiest way to let go of something bad. There is a religious lesson in this. No amount of willpower can shove an idol out of the heart. The reason for this is because the strength of an idol is *love*, that is, perceived goodness. If I live for success, why do I do this? The reason is because the very image of success captivates my heart. I don't have to talk myself into wanting success. To see success is to love it, desire it, and to feel myself driven to pursue it. How then does one resist the mystical gravity of love? The key is to catch sight of something incomparably more lovely. If this new object is sufficiently glorious, the glue that has bound the heart to an idol will dissolve and a new seal, to a new object, will be formed. Such is the magic of captivation.

We can now appreciate how captivation is the solution to dis-attraction, one of the deep problems afflicting men. Men live in a world filled with counterfeit gods. Becoming a Christian does not take them out of this world. Just as married men are called to narrow their vision and to invest their sexual passion in a single woman, in spite of the other options around them, Christians are called to narrow their worship and to invest their spiritual devotion in a single god, in spite of the idols around them. The calling is difficult. The only way ultimately to avoid being taken captive by an idol is to be captivated by Christ. Only Christ's beauty can fortify the heart and insulate it from foreign invasion.[3]

But there is a second benefit of captivation. Captivation empowers. This is due to the nature of love. Love is a renewable resource. It is not depleted as it is used. Even idolatrous love often reveals this. A man who lives for success does not find himself wanting less of success the more he pursues it. The contrary is true. The more he obsesses regarding success, the more he desires it. In this way, love is self-propagating. It fulfills the words of Jesus, 'For to one who has, more will be given' (Matt. 13:12).

Now there is nothing more vital for discipleship than strength. Christianity is not a therapeutic religion whereby men and women are called to release the inner spirit. Christianity is not a secular path to self-fulfillment. Christianity requires discipleship, which is to say *discipline*. There are appetites to be resisted, assignments to be performed, sin to be mortified, precepts to be obeyed, and promises to be believed. We do well to ponder Thomas Watson's statement, 'Though our salvation with regard to Christ is a purchase with regard to us it is a conquest.' Recognizing this, every

---

3.   Benjamin Waugh gives a pithy description of the spiritual power of love in his hymn 'Now Let Us See Thy Beauty, Lord'.

Christian ought to ask the question, 'Where will I get the strength to persevere through all of these difficulties?'

The quick answer is the Holy Spirit. However, this answer needs to be broken down in order to be useful. One of the chief works the Holy Spirit does—in fact the chief work—is to enable believers to search the unsearchable riches of Christ. The reason the Holy Spirit does this is, among other reasons, because the most powerful source of human motivation is captivation. Although there are other motives for Christian obedience such as duty, profit, and fear, none of them produce the enduring power of captivation.[4] These other motives are like simple machines – pulleys, levers, and incline planes. They provide leverage in critical moments of temptation or struggle, but are limited in what they can accomplish. Love as a motivational power is of a whole different order. Love is to fear what a hydraulic lift is to a lever. Once a man is captivated by the glory of Christ he will sacrifice anything, endure anything, to be near to Christ, know Christ, and please Christ. He will declare, 'Whom have I in heaven but you? And there is nothing on earth that I desire besides you' (Ps. 73:25-6).

This is why captivation is of such vital significance to discipleship. The difficulty of traveling to Mars is in part the difficulty of finding a sufficient source of fuel to power a space shuttle the entire way of the journey, there and back. The Christian life is faced with a similar challenge. Where will Christians find the strength to press through combat fatigue and relentlessly advance, decade

---

4. Walter Hilton observes, 'a hound that runs after the hare only because he sees the other hounds running will, when he grows weary, just sit down and rest or turn around and head home. But if he runs because he actually sees the hare, he will not spare himself for weariness until he has it. It is much the same spiritually.' *Toward a Perfect Love*, p. 61.

upon decade, toward the center of holiness? The answer is love. A heart held captive by a vision of Jesus is the only heart that will 'go from strength to strength' through the Valley of Baca, up the mountainside, and on to the gates of Jerusalem (Ps. 84).

This use of captivation ought to be set beside the exhaustion that affects Christian men. Even if life is simplified, a Christian will still find himself tempted to give up on discipleship unless a glorious end is kept in view. Love and gratitude must fuel the journey. The object must be worthy of the quest. The foretastes of living water must be sufficient to motivate a long pilgrimage through the desert. Whoever does not desire Christ above all will not be willing to give up all to have Him. This is no exaggeration. This is the honest truth, a truth that contemporary men need to hear.

Yet, captivation is important for a third reason. Let us not forget the danger of nearsightedness, be it that of David or that of Alexander. What did David need when a beautiful, naked, and available woman crossed his field of vision? He needed a backdrop of the glory of God. A flashlight shines brightly on a moonless night. Under the blaze of a Middle Eastern sun, however, a flashlight is irrelevant. On or off it will go unnoticed. Had David remembered the incomparable pleasures at the right hand of God, he would never have dared sacrifice those joys for a short-lived and guilt-ridden fling. The magnetic field of God's glory would have nullified the attractive power of sin.

Something similar can be said regarding the nearsightedness of Alexander. Remember that, for us, Alexander was a picture of Christian men who overestimate their progress, who relax over time because they are confident in their spiritual attainments. What do such men need? They don't need more assignments. More assignments might only contribute to their pride. What they need is a bigger vision of glory. When I lived in Scotland I used to do a lot of hiking. I would hike up and down mountains and feel pretty good about what I was able to accomplish. However, in Scotland the highest mountain is only about 4,500 feet. Compare that to the tallest mountain in the world which stands over 23,000 feet and my feat is embarrassingly insignificant.

If seen and appreciated with a heart of faith, the glory of God will affect the soul of a man in two ways. First, it will humble a man. Second, it will inspire a man.[5] A man who has beheld a mere spark of God's glory will not weep like Alexander because he has nothing to live for. Rather, he will rejoice with hope knowing that, even within the boundless limits of eternity, the quest of pursuing God will never cease. A man who is captivated by God is a man who has something to live for, *eternally.*

The Objects that Captivate the Eyes of the Heart

What are the sources that ought to captivate the hearts of Christian men? I will mention three. First, the glory of God. There is a radical reorientation of the soul that occurs the moment a man realizes that there is a living God. To read and understand Genesis 1, Psalm 145, the book of Job, or Isaiah 40 is to experience nothing less than a Copernican revolution of the soul. God is all-in-all; I am not. Next to Him even the universe is tiny, simple, and barely getting started. He is there and alive – two facts significant enough to startle the soul into a new spiritual alertness. But there is more: He is also personal, faithful, just, merciful, wise,

---

5. Blaise Pascal is the great commentator on this truth. In the *Pensées* he repeatedly notes how the gospel has the unique ability both to humble pride and to overcome despair. See section 7 in particular.

good, and loving. In a sentence, captivation begins by seeing the footprint of a Creator in the Old Testament and then realizing that this trace is in fact a Holy Presence addressing me *right now*.[6] The effect of such an encounter is to fall on one's face and to worship in reverent silence.[7]

Second, captivation occurs when a heart beholds the beauty of Christ. In *The Religious Affections* Jonathan Edwards makes the point that, in saving us, God orchestrated our redemption so that it would be both effective and beautiful.[8] Such is the wondrous power of the cross. The very act that saves us captivates the wellspring of our devotion. Men who are prepared for spiritual growth have tasted this beauty. They understand that the greatest honor and delight available to human beings is knowledge of God through Jesus Christ. Jesus and Jesus alone is 'the radiance of God's glory and the exact imprint of His nature' (Heb. 1:3). He is the light of God's presence and the fountain of joy (Ps. 36; John 1:4). Knowing Him, and the Father through Him, is eternal life (John 17:3).[9]

---

6. C. S. Lewis powerfully describes his first encounter with the living presence of God in *Surprised by Joy*. He says, 'As the dry bones shook and came together in that dreadful Valley of Ezekiel's, so now a philosophical theorem, cerebrally entertained, began to stir and heave and throw off its grave-clothes, and stood upright and became a living presence. I was allowed to play with philosophy no longer.'

7. Isaac Watt's hymn 'Eternal Power! Whose High Abode' ends with the stanza: 'God is in heaven and men below;/ Be short our tunes, our words be few;/ A sacred reverence checks our songs,/ And praise sits silent on our tongues.'

8. See Jonathan Edwards, *The Religious Affections* (Edinburgh: Banner of Truth, 2001).

9. If any men would like to step into the heart of a man fully captivated by the beauty of Christ, they should read the letters of Samuel Rutherford. The letters are available online.

In case this sounds idealistic allow me to clarify one point. What I am describing is hunger, not consistency. A man who has beheld Christ will still struggle against sin and waver in his loyalty. Sinful appetites will frequently distract him from his first love. After all, did not David, even David—the great lover of God—fall into the pettiest of sin? If the man who penned the words 'your love is better than life' (Ps. 63) struggled against temptation, so shall we. But there is a more profound lesson to learn from David than our proclivity to sin. As Thomas Brooks notes, David is not so much an example of extraordinary sin as he is an example of extraordinary repentance.[10] The depth of David's grief was greater than the height of his sin. Why was this? The answer is because David's heart was captivated by a love for God. David knew where the fountain of living water was, and once he realized that he had forsaken this for broken cisterns, his stony heart crumbled in repentance.

Something similar is true for any man who has beheld of the beauty of Christ. To be captivated by Christ is not to be finished with sin. Yet to be captivated is to long for the day when Christ sweeps the last crumb of leaven from the heart. Any man who is captivated will readily sing the words of William Cowper:

> *The dearest idol I have known,*
> *Whate're that idol be,*
> *Help me to tear it from thy throne,*
> *And worship only thee.*[11]

The final source of captivation is a vision of the glory of godliness. There is nothing uglier to the eyes of unbelief than a radical pursuit

---

10. Thomas Brooks, *Precious Remedies*.

11. From the hymn, 'O for a closer walk with God'.

of holiness. Submission instead of assertion, meekness instead of pride, self-control instead of self-fulfillment, persecution instead of comfort, heavenly treasure instead of earthly reward, spiritual joy instead of momentary pleasure – this reads like a blueprint for misery to a secular audience. But the captivated man has a different point of view. To him, the gain of godliness far outweighs the costs. To follow the way of the cross is to venture down a path that leads to eternal joy, honor, and fellowship. Are there difficulties? Yes. Are there sacrifices? Of course. But there is also imperishable, undefiled, and unfading *blessing* (1 Pet. 1:4). A captivated man appreciates the words of Isaac Watts, 'Religion never was designed to make our pleasure less.' He knows that the glory outweighs the shame, the hope infinitely repays the sacrifice. For him, the way of the cross is the only path through life that could satisfy his deepest longings. Such a man appreciates the reply of Peter to Jesus when Jesus asked the twelve if they would like to go a different way: 'Lord, to whom should we go? You have the words of eternal life' (John 6:68).

The Measurables of Captivation

How does a man know if his heart is captivated? There are four tests that reveal when a heart has tasted the glory of God. The first is the test of submission. A man who has seen something of the splendor of holiness will be willing to profess the words that Ittai the Gittite spoke to David, 'As the Lord lives, and as the lord my king lives, wherever my lord the kings shall be, whether for death or for life, there also will your servant be' (2 Sam. 15:21). A captivated man is willing to endure hardship in order to be near to Christ. The second is the test of sacrifice. Why was Abraham willing to place Isaac, his beloved son, on the altar? The reason was because Abraham worshiped a glorious God from whom nothing could be withheld. A true lover of God will not keep anything from his Lord. Such a man knows enough of God to believe the words of the hymn, 'But we never will prove/the delights of his love/until all on the altar we lay'. The third is the test of satisfaction. Walter Hilton says to his reader, 'I shall offer you one word to cover all that it is you ought to see, desire, and find – for in this word is all you have lost. This word is *Jesus*.'[12] The captivated man has tasted and seen the truth of this word. He knows that Christ alone satisfies the longings of the heart. Finally, there is the test of sorrow. One thought pierces the heart of a lover of God more deeply than any other: the thought that I might dishonor the Father, grieve the Spirit, and betray the Son. For the captivated man sin is not an inconvenience; it is a horror. With David, he confesses, 'Against you, you alone, have I sinned.' Maintaining communion with God is the great aim of life that he pursues with earnestness and care.

---

12. Walter Hilton, *Toward a Perfect* Love, p. 73.

Men Need Clarity

◁◁◁◆◆◆▷▷▷

I magine that you and I live in England during the early 1900s. Patriotism is fierce. We are gripped by the glory of the Empire, and we long for an opportunity to carry a rifle in the name of our king. Suddenly, WWI breaks outs, and we find ourselves in line along with thousands of other young men, waiting to enlist in the armed forces. We are passionate, but we are also ignorant. We have no idea what trench warfare is or of the nature of new technologies about to be introduced to the battlefield. We think we are gallant knights joining a glorious crusade; in fact, we are sheep heading to a slaughterhouse.

Captivation without clarity, deep emotion without knowledge, is dangerous. This is true in everyday life; it is also true in spiritual life. Ignorance is a grave threat to spirituality. If men do not have a clear and true perspective of the Christian life, they will not understand what they are attempting, and thus the attempt itself will be naive and ill-measured. They will foolishly charge forward like the Light Brigade with no ability to determine what is wise and what is futile.

Defining Clarity

By clarity I mean a broad and true perspective on the Christian life. To understand this, picture a man walking down a path in the woods. The trail is new to him, and he does not know where he is or where he is going. There is a light fog and, between the mist and the thick undergrowth of trees and bushes, visibility is minimal. He can only see the next thirty yards in front of him.

Suddenly, the path begins to climb uphill. After several minutes it bends sharply to the left. The man finds himself perched at the top of a hill, the mist gone, and the broad landscape visible around him. He catches a glimpse of where he is going, the path before him, and some of the difficulties soon to be encountered. This is what I mean by clarity. A man with clarity is a man who has an accurate sense of the landscape of discipleship.

There are certain telltale markers of men without clarity. Most importantly, such men are negligent, confused, and frustrated. They are negligent because they are not aware of the dangers around them. If the devil is a clown, sin, a nuisance, and the world, a playground, there is little reason to be wary. They are confused because they are not able to make sense of the path they are on. The Christian life feels more like a treadmill to them than a purposeful climb. They are frustrated because the journey feels more difficult than it needs to be. Deep down, like Job, they long to question God's leadership. Could not an easier path have been chosen?

Likewise, a man with clarity is readily identifiable. The fruit he bears is alertness, understanding, and focus. He is alert because he sees the dangers ahead, and he knows that any loss of sobriety will be a grave risk to his safety. He has understanding insofar as he appreciates that every leg of the journey is purposeful and necessary in order to reach the final destination. He is focused for the very same reason that another is frustrated: the path is challenging and requires the sum of his energy to endure.

An entire book could be written on clarity. Yet, we need not get lost in the vastness of the topic. Our emphasis is on the imperative, not on the ideal. The question we need to answer is governed by necessity: what clarity do men *most need* in order to be prepared for spiritual growth?

Vital Areas of Clarity

First, men need clarity regarding the *final destination of life*. Generally, life is lived according to one of two models, as a quest or as a pilgrimage. The difference between these two patterns is worth pondering.

Within a quest, ambiguity is part of the journey. A knight goes out in search of the Holy Grail, but he has little to no idea what the grail looks like or where to find it. Most of his energy is spent looking for clues rather than pursuing clear objectives. He often gets waylaid, and side adventures end up being as important in the long run as the original task itself.

Most Christian men today live their lives in this way.[13] They have some fuzzy idea in their head regarding what they are after ('God', 'happiness', 'peace', 'holiness', 'fulfillment'), but each concept is too ambiguous to be meaningful. They wander, in part, because they are distracted and, in part, because they lack concrete direction. To take an example, until a man has a clear idea regarding what 'peace' or 'fulfillment' is, he will not be able to mount a full spirited attempt to go and chase it. The same is true of 'holiness' or 'godliness'. If men look as if they are drifting from one well to another, in search of living water, the reason is because *they are*. Without a fixed destination, wandering is the most productive thing that a man can do.

---

13. David Brooks discusses the contemporary tendency to view life as a quest in *The Social Animal,* p. 190-192. For a deeper reflection on this theme see Paul Ricoeur, 'Life in Quest of Narrative' in *On Paul Ricoeur: Narrative and Interpretation*, ed. David Wood (New York: Routledge, 2002).

A pilgrimage is different from a quest because, within a pilgrimage, the destination is as definite as a home address. The pilgrim knows precisely what he is after. Wake him up in the middle of the night with the question, 'Where are you going?' and he will unflinchingly give the answer. There may be surprises along the way, and mistaken diversions that delay progress, but the final goal is specific and incontestable.

Men who desire spiritual maturity need to live their lives as pilgrimages, not quests. They need to know with precision what the final destination of life is. It is not enough to say 'holiness' or 'union with Christ'. Terms must be defined. Theological ideas must be described. If I tell a man to go to Scotland, he will look at me and ask, where should I go *in Scotland*? If I add, travel to the Highlands, he will reply, *where*? If, finally, I clarify, 'Go to the Free Church, Camault Muir, Kiltarlity,' no further questions will be required. The man will have all the information he needs to travel to the front door of a church I used to pastor.

Having a clear destination is no less important in life than it is on a road trip. Men do not need to be sent to park benches to contemplate the meaning of life. They need to be given detailed coordinates. They do not need to gaze into their navels looking for a mysterious purpose. They need to be told unequivocally that the judgment seat of Christ is the final stop of every bus, and that the chief objective of each individual life is 'to walk in a manner worthy of the Lord, fully pleasing to him, bearing fruit in every good work and increasing in the knowledge of God' (Col. 1:10). For any reader of the New Testament, there is no excuse for running aimlessly. There is no reason to beat the air. The Bible has revealed a finishing line so that each can run, like an athlete, to win the prize (1 Cor. 9:24).

No one has captured the power of viewing life as a pilgrimage as memorably as John Bunyan. The whole of *Pilgrim's Progress* demonstrates the way in which clarity and determination go hand-in-hand. The clearer I see the final goal, the more doggedly I can pursue it. The great pilgrim hymn by Bunyan captures this truth perfectly:

Who would true Valour see
Let him come hither;
One here will Constant be,
Come Wind, come Weather.
There's no Discouragement,
Shall make him once Relent,
His first avow'd Intent,
To be a Pilgrim.

Who so beset him round,
With dismal Storys,
Do but themselves Confound;
His Strength the more is.
No Lyon can him fright,
He'l with a Gyant Fight,
But he will have a right,
To be a Pilgrim.

Hobgoblin, nor foul Fiend,
Can daunt his Spirit:
He knows, he at the end,
Shall Life Inherit.
Then Fancies fly away,
He'l fear not what men say,
He'l labour Night and Day,
To be a Pilgrim.

Constancy, intentionality, relentlessness, fortitude, diligence, resolve – these are the virtues that result from seeing life as a pilgrimage. Such virtues are essential for men who are hungry for spiritual growth.

Second, in addition to the destination of life, men also need clarity regarding the path to maturity. When some men think of discipleship they think of church buildings, lecture halls, leadership training programs, seminaries, and prayer closets. Discipleship, in their minds, is something that occurs detached from normal life. They imagine that discipleship is for Christians what school is for children. Discipleship is formal, routine, part-time, and set apart from the rest of life. This mindset is unhelpful. In truth, discipleship is not for Christians what school is for children; discipleship is for Christians what being educated is for children.[14] The education of a child never stops. All of the time, at home, in school, among friends, and in between, a child is being educated (for better or worse). He is always learning what it means to participate in the world around him and shaping his character accordingly. Something similar is true for Christians. When is God not teaching us? *Never.* Every situation, every activity, every responsibility is an opportunity for growth. Normal life in the everyday world – this is the most important classroom in which Christians are trained.

This widening of the circle of discipleship is important for understanding the road to maturity. If we think of discipleship as a limited activity, then the road to maturity will be confined to a narrow set of disciplines like Bible study, prayer, and fellowship.

---

14.   The English word education comes from the Latin word *educare*, which literally means 'to lead out'. An education is far more than preparation for a job. To be educated is to be prepared to step into reality and to find a place, not only in society, but before God.

However, if the circle of discipleship is expanded, our perspective is changed. Discipleship contains no less than it did before, but it does contain more.

This backdrop is necessary in order to clarify for men the nature of the path that leads to spiritual maturity. The path is neither a method, nor a technique, nor a curriculum, nor a program. The path, rather, is best described by the following experiences: hard work, unanticipated trials, unavoidable suffering, uncomfortable assignments, difficult relationships, and simple routines. This is the stuff that more than anything else produces long-term growth among Christians.

Why is this? Consider the example of hard work. I have yet to meet a man who reached spiritual maturity by reading the verse of the day on his phone. Maturity is a product of memorizing the Word, meditating on the Word, studying the Word, hearing the Word, and singing the Word. Mature men of God are men whose blood is Bibline, to use Bunyan's choice phrase. Cut them open and the Word of God comes out. Men need to appreciate that there are no elevators to eliminate the spiritual equivalent of climbing stairs. A man must harden his knees in prayer if he wants to have an intimate knowledge of God. He must read lots of books if he wants to have a Christian perspective on culture. He must take a spade to his heart if he wants to dig up the roots of sin. Hard work cannot be avoided. Spiritual fruit, like natural fruit, requires the sweat of the brow.

Men deserve to hear the same level of candidness when thinking about trials, suffering, assignments, and relationships. Regardless of what is said in some churches, men need to re-read the New Testament, looking at the experiences of Jesus' earliest followers as an example of what Christians ought to expect today. The reason for this is that God's methods then were not accidental. There are lessons learned through suffering that cannot be taught through prosperity. The anvil of a severe trial forges a toughness of virtue that cannot be wrought through times of ease. Faith will never achieve the totality of trust until Christians are pressed into the space of daring obedience. Much of the fruit of the Spirit—love, joy, peace, patience, kindness, goodness, gentleness, and self-control—grows best, not in the delicious climate of mutual affection, but under the harsh rays of awkward, even painful, relationships. Men need to understand that following Jesus is not a small thing, like adopting a set of spiritual routines. Discipleship is far more like enlisting in the military than taking up a hobby. Someone else is now in charge of my life, and He is willing to do whatever it takes to make sure that the finished product is of the highest order.

Why am I putting the difficulties of discipleship in the fore-ground instead of its joys? Is my goal to be a wet blanket? No, I do so for one reason: men deserve to hear the truth. The basic under-standing of all Christians up until the nineteenth century was that the only way to persevere into the kingdom was by a kind of 'holy violence'.[15] This sobriety, this realism, has been lost today, like the law of God before the reign of Josiah. Do men need to hear about the glories, and privileges, and honors of following Jesus? Of course they do. Yet, from most pulpits these jewels are brought out and put on public display every Sunday. What is left hidden in the back closet is the sword and the trowel, the reminders that only by fighting and toil is maturity won.

There are two further areas where men are in desperate need of clarity. First, they need a truthful perspective on the threats

---

15. On 'holy violence' see Thomas Watson, *The Christian Soldier.*

that they will encounter as disciples of Christ. Indwelling sin, the devil, and the world are not relics of a superstitious age. They are a triumvirate of evil that imperil the footsteps of a man every moment of every day. To be ignorant of indwelling sin is more dangerous than to be ignorant of cancer. To ignore the devil is as hazardous as stepping into the cage of a hungry lion. To relax in the presence of the world is like sleeping in a cave with a band of terrorists. Spiritual combat is real. If men do not believe this they will not have the watchfulness required to survive.

But finally men need to appreciate the resources that God has given them, not only to be strengthened in the face of the enemy, but to overcome the fiercest of temptations. The Word is precisely what God says it is: a double-edged sword to be wielded in the face of the devil. Prayer is nothing less than a direct line of communication between me and the omnipotent ruler of the universe. The Spirit of God is the presence of Christ in me, His resurrected power, His eternal wisdom, and His inviolable life. Baptism and the Lord's Table are a ring on the finger and a multicolored robe on the back, reminding us that, from the ceiling of heaven to the floor of hell, nothing can sever the children of God from the love of God.

In summary, destination, road, threats, and resources – if a man has a clear perspective on these his mind will be girded and ready for growth. He will not be taken captive by the secularism of the unbelieving world or by the cheap grace of consumeristic churches. Instead, he will see life for what it is:

> *If we have died with him, we will also live with*
> *   him;*
> *If we endure with him, we will also reign with*
> *   him;*

If we deny him, he will also deny us;
If we are faithless, he remains faithful – for he
cannot deny himself

(2 Tim. 2:11-13).

The Benefits of Clarity

Why is clarity such a vital condition for spiritual growth? One reason is because clarity contests sloth. By sloth I mean something more than laziness. Traditionally, sloth is one of seven deadly sins. Sloth is a reluctance to be persistent in spiritual disciplines. Because of slothfulness the heart of faith grows feeble before God, not because God is unwilling to supply grace, but because a Christian avoids the supply lines where grace is freely on offer.

In section one we saw the way in which the vice of slothfulness was reinforced by warped beliefs. A lot of contemporary Christians do not believe that growth requires effort. They do not think that life is a battlefield. They have been spoon-fed a steady diet of cheap grace and self-fulfillment and, as a result, have little incentive to invest in spiritual fitness. If a man is going to sit all day in a plush office chair he feels no need to run wind sprints or do squats. If a man is expected to carry a football through a seam of 300-pound defensive linemen, his attitude is different. Something similar is true for Christians. To attain clarity is to view life from the perspective of spiritual combat. Once a man understands this, spiritual training will not be viewed as an interesting elective, but as a requirement for survival. He will appreciate that to walk up and down the streets of this world without knowing the Word of God is every bit as reckless as storming an enemy camp unarmed. To skip prayer for a single day is like stepping behind enemy lines without taking the time to put on body armor. Alertness and diligence depend upon a true perspective. Until a man has clarity, he cannot help but be negligent.

Furthermore, clarity gives hope. None of the apostles hold their punches when it comes to talking about the afflictions, trials, and suffering that Christians will experience. And yet somehow nearly every passage that zooms in on suffering ends up zooming out on joy or hope. The examples are numerous. Paul tells us to 'rejoice in our sufferings' because they ultimately lead to glory (Rom. 5:1-5, 8:18-25). Hebrews informs us not to fret the painful discipline of God because the outcome will be 'the peaceful fruit of righteousness' (12:3-11). James says, 'Count it all joy, my brothers, when you meet trials of various kind for you know that the testing of your faith produces steadfastness' (1:2-3). Peter encourages new Christians to continue to rejoice in being grieved by 'various trials' because the difficulties are a God-appointed fire to purify the hearts of the faithful. The question every Christian man needs to ask is, how is this alchemy performed? What is it that enables the sediment of suffering to be transformed into the rich alloy of joyful hope? The answer is clarity. What Paul, Hebrews, James, and Peter all have in common is a clear perspective of the big picture of life. They are not surprised by affliction; they are not unsettled by difficulties. The cross has given them a simple filter by which to understand the most painful of experiences: for those trusting in Christ, *suffering leads to glory.*

Finally, clarity enables fellowship. How is it that Christians are able to comfort each other, to encourage each other, and to stir up one another to love and good works? The answer is, to a large degree, because they share the same perspective on life. Spiritual friends are friends who are traveling according to the same itinerary. The circumstances of each life might differ, but the overall pattern is the same. Clarity, which is another name for *seeing this pattern*, is a glue that binds the heart of one believer to that of another. Once you and I both realize that the instructions I am following are the same as yours, a spirit of fellowship erupts like a flame from kindling. Suddenly, I know something very intimate about you even as you know something personal about me. We are no longer strangers; we are comrades. Clarity helps to form this bond.

The Measurables of Clarity

How does a man know when a degree of clarity is attained? 1 Peter 1:13 offers an answer. Peter writes, 'Therefore, girding up the loins of your mind, and being sober-minded, set your hope fully on the grace that will be brought to you at the revelation of Christ Jesus'. Three traits are evident in this verse. The first is readiness. A man with clarity is watchful and ready for action (c.f. Luke 12:35-48). He is a soldier on duty, not a civilian at ease (2 Tim. 2:4). Second is sobriety. His mind is not lulled into sleep by the superficial safety and comfort of the modern world. He has his wits about him. He knows that the enemy is lurking and that to risk complacency is to risk injury. The third trait is simplicity, a total investment of hope in the final unveiling of Christ. For the man with clarity, there are only two days: *this day*, the one I am living, and *that Day*, the day when I bow before the throne of Jesus. Viewed from this perspective, the agenda of life is simple: to serve Christ. Simplicity is therefore the offspring of clarity.

Men Need Camaraderie

◁◁◁◆◆◆▷▷▷

Observing Christians I am often reminded of lions. Among lions the females go out and work together to take down wildebeest, zebra, and other prey. The males, meanwhile, sit by themselves, each one with his head held high, venting a proud air of independence. A similar phenomenon occurs in churches across the world. Women are busy collaborating on projects of feeding the homeless, mentoring the young, and studying the Bible. Instinctively, they seem to feel a need for one another. Men, on the other hand, are disengaged and aloof. They gather together on rare occasions—usually if bacon is cooked—but, otherwise, they act as if spiritual isolation is in the fabric of their DNA.

Men are Social Animals

Among men, the drum cannot be beaten too loudly that human beings are social animals. We might think of ourselves as stately oaks set apart from each other on a broad and open landscape. However, the truth is that we are more like branches on a single tree, each one dependent on others for sap and nourishment. This sociological fact is also a spiritual fact. No factor influences the development of a man more than the circle of people he calls his friends. To see them—their aspirations, their values, their worldview, their practices—is to see himself.[16] To be around them is to step into a kiln and to be hardened into their likeness.

Given our social nature, a man who is passive regarding friendship is a fool. According to Aelred of Rievaulx, the great medieval writer on spiritual friendship, close relationships with other Christians do the following: cultivate virtue, assail vice, temper adversity, moderate prosperity, give joy, and lead to Christ.[17] If a man is serious about spiritual maturity, these advantages cannot be ignored. This is why camaraderie is an essential condition for growth. John Rambo might be an exciting hero for a Hollywood script, but there are no Rambos in the kingdom of God. No soldier of Christ is so complete in himself that he should risk facing the enemy on his own. As Marshall noted in *Men against Fire*, soldiers function best when placed in fire-teams. They need constant communication, mutual support, and the simple childlike security of knowing that, regardless of how fierce the battle gets, *I am not alone.*

Part of the difficulty of talking about friendship with men is that most guys think that they already know what friendship is. Making friends, after all, is something that human beings do naturally. We begin to form close relationships before we have any idea what we are doing. Thus many assume that friendship is like walking, something that normal people can figure out without much detailed instruction.

This may be true of some types of friendship, but not for spiritual friendship. Spiritual friendship is more like learning to ride a bicycle

16. On this aspect of identity see Paul Ricoeur, *Oneself as Another* trans. Kathleen Bailey (Chicago: University of Chicago Press, 1992), p. 121.

17. Aelred of Rievaulx, *Spiritual Friendship* trans. M. Eugenia Laker (Notre Dame: Ave Maria, 2008), pp. 58-63.

than learning to walk. Teaching and practice are required. The basic motions might be familiar, but they are put together in new and more complicated patterns. Therefore, men do need instruction about the mechanics of spiritual friendship. But, in truth, they need something even more basic. They need to know *what spiritual friendship is.*

The Marks of Spiritual Camaraderie

There are three distinguishing marks of spiritual friendship. The first is *right intention*. Intention is not characteristic of most types of friendships. Men need to understand this. When most men think of friendship they tend to think of a single category. In truth, there are multiple types of friendship: there are friendships based on affection (think high school classmates); there are friendships based on pleasure (think golf buddies); and there are friendships based on utility (work colleagues). In none of these relationships does intention factor in as a primary element of the relationship.

Spiritual friendship is different. The relationship is welded together by a shared vision of excellence, of glory, of blessing. This vision creates a spirit of intentionality within the relationship. Unlike high school classmates who are happy to reminisce about the past, or golf buddies who only want to have fun on the weekend, spiritual friends are like athletes in training. They band together because each edges the other onto glory and because both know that, joined together, they will advance further toward perfection than either could alone.

Yet, intentionality, by itself, is insufficient to produce spiritual friendship. The intent must be *right*. Spiritual friends are comrades who join together in pursuit of Christ. The following words of Paul are an apt description of the basic intent that drives one Christian to partner with another: 'That I may know him and the power of his resurrection, and may share in his sufferings, becoming like him in his death, that by any means possible I may attain the resurrection from the dead' (Phil. 3:10-11). Knowing Christ, obeying Christ, being conformed to Christ – these are the objectives pursued in spiritual friendship. Aelred beautifully captures this in his own lyrical words: 'And thus, friend cleaving to friend in the spirit of Christ, is made with Christ but one heart and one soul, and so mounting aloft through degrees of love to friendship with Christ, he is made one spirit with him.'[18] Union with Christ, that is the intent that distinguishes spiritual friendship from every other kind.

The second mark of spiritual friendship is a *shared thermostat.* I hope never to repeat the frustration of living in an apartment with a bunch of unmarried men. Among the difficulties is the challenge of setting the thermostat. Whereas one room-mate would attempt to replicate the weather conditions of the North Pole, another would mistake our apartment for a sweat lodge. The result was often a dangerous hive of passive-aggressiveness.

Spiritual friendship requires shared consent regarding the desired temperature of discipleship. Different Christians have different interpretations of what it means to be a devout follower of Jesus. Some are happy to exist in a tepid, lukewarm state. Others feel the need to kick-start the burner whenever the boil drops to a simmer. Spiritual friendship is distinct from other Christian relationships because spiritual appetites must be in sync. Such

---

18. Aelred, *Spiritual Friendship*, p. 62.

friends not only share a sense of where they are going, but there is a pace, an earnestness, that all hope to maintain.

Why is a shared thermostat so important? Any competitive athlete can give the answer. Drive is contagious. We not only pick up the spiritual habits of our inner circle of friends, we feed off their energy. Next to captivation, there is no source of motivation among Christians more powerful than spiritual friendship. This insight is not new. In Ecclesiastes we read, 'If two lie together, they keep warm, but how can one keep warm alone?' (4:11).

The third trait of spiritual friendship is a *covenant agreement.* There are two sides to this agreement. On the one hand, *I* agree to open the windows and doors of my life so that *you* can see the inner workings of my heart. Does this mean that everything inside of me is exposed? Of course not. The point is not that every drawer gets emptied, the content being dumped in the light of the sun. Boredom (on the part of the listener) and narcissism (on the part of the speaker) is reason enough to avoid this. The point, rather, is that no closet is locked to bar entry. I state my intention to live in the light rather than in the darkness and to resist the powers of shame, guilt, and fear that would cause me to hide what needs to be laid bare.

On the other hand, I give you permission to speak truth to me in love. In the book *Building Your Band of Brothers*, Stephen Mansfield talks about the importance of setting up what he calls a 'free-fire zone'.[19] A free-fire zone is a mutual commitment to one another, or to all members of a small band, that anything which needs to be said will be said for the sake of a higher good. Within spiritual friendship, cowardice

---

19. Stephen Mansfield, *Building Your Band of Brothers* (Nashville: Blackwatch Digital, 2016), pp. 47-65.

must be resisted. To permit a man to veer off the path of righteousness is an act of hatred, not love. While friends must avoid being pugnacious, censorious, and nit-picky, they must also avoid being passive, permissive, and complacent. No spiritual friendship is genuine unless everyone involved is committed to speaking the truth, even if it stings.[20]

How important is spiritual friendship, *really*? The more men I speak to the smaller the percentage appears to be that has anything like the camaraderie I am describing. The general assumption seems to be that the recipe of church membership, participation in a small group, and a Christian spouse (at least among the married) ought to be sufficient to support spiritual growth. I think this is dangerously naive. I am convinced that spiritual friendship is not an extra layer of icing that can or cannot be lathered over a cake. Spiritual friendship is an ingredient of the cake itself—like butter, salt, or sugar—which, if left out, affects the product as a whole. House groups are an important balance to large church gatherings, but they are too porous and diverse to enable a covenant agreement. A believing spouse is one of the greatest gifts that God can provide. But just as a house requires more than one load-bearing wall, so do Christian lives. To lean entirely on a wife for spiritual support is unfair to her and unwise for him. There are real differences between being a man and being a woman, and men need men just as women need women.

The Benefits of Spiritual Friendship

Affirmation should not be undervalued. The word affirmation is abused in pop psychology, but abuse does not merit abandonment. Many a Christian man will step each day into a workplace in which he is the

---

20.   For the nuts and bolts of how to do this see Dietrich Bonhoeffer, *Life Together*, trans. John Doberstein (London: SCM, 1954), pp. 69-85.

only person around him whose life goal is to know, serve, and delight in the Lord Jesus Christ. He will feel like an exile in a foreign land, trying to maintain an identity that is threatened by the culture around him. In such arid conditions, the vitality of faith begins to evaporate, drop by drop, day by day. Zeal will cool; focus will relax; resolve will weaken. Just as plants need water, human beings need affirmation. For identity to be maintained we need, regularly, to look into the eyes of a circle of people who reflect back to us our deep loves, our guiding aspirations, and our distinct point of view. Spiritual friends provide this. A man does not need a throng of people to affirm the root of his identity. He needs a few, select voices who will confirm to him in moments of self-doubt that he is headed in the right direction.

Spiritual friendship also provides inspiration. It is often said that a man is the average of his five best friends. There is much truth to this. Who we run with determines the pace we keep. This is why a shared thermostat is so important. The idea of a thermostat is that, if the temperature drops too low, the heating will kick-on. The purpose is consistency. Due to our sinful nature every Christian is prone to drifting, relaxing, holding back, distraction, and giving up in the face of difficulty. Inconsistency is natural to us; consistency is an ongoing struggle. What can a man do to protect himself from such weakness? There is no guardrail more useful than a circle of spiritual friends. Hearing such words as 'Don't give up!', 'Where were you?', 'You can do all things through Christ who strengthens you', or 'Fear not! God is with you', can be a cup of Gatorade on a hot day, refreshing the heart and supplying strength for yet another leg of the race.

Finally, spiritual friendship enables accountability. We need to recall that two of the chief problems restricting the growth of men are nearsightedness and distraction. The difficulty with both of these is that a person is partially unconscious of what is going on. By the time David was contemplating a night with Bathsheba his blood was already boiling. Lust had already mounted a siege against the conscience and was catapulting missiles against the will. What would have been the very best safety valve for David while he was pacing the decking of his palace? He should have had Abiathar the priest, or Nathan the prophet, or some other man of God walking with him. A good friend would have smacked him across the face and told him to recollect the life of Saul before dabbling in sin.

Distraction is similar. We don't distract ourselves. Something else distracts us. Work gets busy and all of a sudden every mental faculty is focused on meeting a deadline rather than abiding in Christ. We get caught in the current of life and suddenly realize that youth athletics has replaced worship as the focus of Sundays. How can we protect ourselves so that we realize our mistakes before drifting a mile down river? No method is more useful than walking closely with a band of other men. They will spot errors before we do. They will see the plank in the eye that otherwise is blinding.

The stakes of righteousness are far too high to venture through life alone. All of us teeter on the edge of a fall that could ruin our marriages, embitter our children, and defame the name of God. We need more than soft accountability; we need hard accountability. We need friends who are willing to draw a line in the sand and to warn us against crossing it. If Aaron, David, Solomon, and Peter stumbled into wicked rebellion, what makes us think that we can walk through the streets of Sodom undefiled? Men who are serious about discipleship need more than a passionate heart and a well-trained mind. They need comrades who care enough about them to tell them, *no!* A single chord is easily broken. It is only by weaving it among others that it becomes strong.

Men Need Competence

◁◁◁◆◆◆▷▷▷

Competence is not a word used often in church. The preferred word is 'equipped'. There are equipping ministries, midweek gatherings called 'Equip', and regular conferences organized around the call in Ephesians 4:12 'to equip the saints for the work of ministry.' All of this is good. Nonetheless, I sometimes wonder if the focus of a lot of these activities is slightly skewed. Think for a moment about the word 'equipped'. What does it mean to be equipped? A man who is equipped for a long journey is a man who has all of the necessary supplies. His clothes are packed. He has sufficient food and water. He has a compass, a map, and adequate camping supplies. Materially, nothing is lacking that would be needed for the venture. But here is the problem: a man could be equipped without being competent. He might have a compass, but he might not know how to use one. He might have camping supplies, but he might not know how to start a fire in the wild, how to cook outdoors, or how to store his food so that wild animals cannot reach it.

Learning Versus Teaching

My interpretation of the word 'equipped' might not be entirely correct; however, I believe the underlying point is important to grasp.

There are a lot of Christians who are equipped for the Christian life, but who are not competent. They have Bibles and other Bible study resources at home, but they do not know how to handle rightly the Word of truth (2 Tim. 2:15). They attend church with spotless regularity. But they do not know how to participate meaningfully in corporate worship, how to listen well to a sermon, or how to stir up other Christians to love and good deeds (Heb. 10:24-25). The list could go on and on. The problem is not that Christians materially lack the stuff in their life that would promote growth. The problem is that they are unskilled in using, applying, or participating in the resources that are within arm's reach.

I think the cause of the problem is highlighted by a provocative question that Peter Drucker, the doyen of management theory in the twentieth century, once asked while conversing with Albert Shanker, who at the time was a leader in the field of education. In the midst of the exchange Drucker interrupted Shanker with a eureka insight: 'For hundreds of years, then, our emphasis has been on how well the teachers teach rather than on how well the students learn?'[21] This was the precise point that Shanker had been trying to make. He had been trying to communicate the degree to which modern schools were built around the needs of teachers, not around the needs of students. The goal had been effective teaching, not effective learning.[22]

The same problem is evident in the equipping ministries of a lot of churches. The evidence for this is that almost all of formal 'discipleship'

---

21. The conversation can be found in Peter Drucker, *Managing the Non-Profit Organization: Principles and Practices*, Part 3, section 4 (Kindle edition) (New York: HarpersCollins, 2010).

22. This idea is explored in much greater detail by Neil Postman and Charles Weingartner in *Teaching as a Subversive Activity* (New York: Delta, 1969).

takes place in either a lecture hall (sanctuary) or classroom. The reason for this is obvious: lecture halls and classrooms are convenient spaces *to teach*. The challenge is that what is useful for teaching is not always adequate for learning. Learning, after all, requires more than teaching. Ordinary experience gives plenty of evidence of this. In most cases, becoming proficient in any skill requires at least four stages of learning: directing, showing, supporting, and delegating.[23] If I want to learn how to frame a house, attending lectures, at most, can only be a part of the process. Along with verbal instruction I need someone to show me how to perform the basic actions; I need someone to watch me as I try to put a wall together myself; and I need someone who will delegate sufficient responsibility to me so that, as I continue to practice the skill, I can achieve proficiency.

The point is this: men need more than teaching. They need more than equipping. They need *competence*. The test of competence is not how well I was taught, but how well I have learned. I can attend an 'equipping church', but still be an incompetent disciple. The question raised by competence is this, 'Do I have the basic knowledge and skills required for discipleship?' If the answer is 'no', my freedom to mature will be restricted.

Why Men Need Competence

Competence reinforces motivation. Recall the story of me as a teenager feeling paralyzed because I was supposed to paint the exterior of a house, but had no idea how to do so. Think of the difference it would have made if an older guy had come along

---

23. For an example of how these principles can be applied to Christian discipleship see Randy Pope, *Insourcing: Bringing Discipleship Back to the Local Church* (Grand Rapids: Zondervan, 2013).

to show me the very simple techniques involved with scraping, caulking, and painting. Such 'coaching' would not have made the job fun or the task easy. However, the instruction would have alleviated the mental distress and frustration that had bottle-necked my motivation.

There are a lot of men who are hindered from Bible study, or dealing with sin, or evangelism, or prayer, for reasons that are similar to why I struggled to paint a house. They feel a nausea that is caused not by unwillingness, but uncertainty. They avoid the prayer closet because no one has taught them to pray. They keep the Bible closed because no one has taught them how to open it. Competence does not remove the hard work that is involved in discipleship. However, it can alleviate the paralysis that results from feeling inadequate. To keep a ball rolling, two things are needed: impetus from behind and an open path before. Competence may not create the motivation, or impetus, that is required to keep a disciple moving. However, competence goes a long way to clearing the road ahead so that a man feels able and unrestricted.[24]

Another benefit of competence is effective action. Now I must be careful in using the word effective. Every millimeter of Christian growth is due to the grace of God. Therefore, no action can be effective in the sense that it guarantees progress. And yet, as always, there are two extremes to avoid. Along with recognizing our dependence on grace we must also admit that there are wise practices and foolish

---

24. Dawson Trotman's biographer notes that one of his fundamental insights regarding discipleship was that 'the gap between desire and fulfillment in the lives of many who sincerely wanted to grow in Christ and follow Him could be bridged by simply giving them the tools for success and teaching them to use them.' See Betty Skinner, *Daws*, p. 145.

practices, paths that have been tried and proven and paths that have been sealed off as dead ends.

When attempting any new activity, be it a sport, learning a musical instrument, or engaging in the Christian life, it is always wise to learn the wisdom that has been accumulated and passed down through generations of experience. A man can pick up a guitar and try to teach himself. If he is motivated and works hard, he might be able to make a lot of progress. However, the most effective method of mastering an instrument is not to chart a new path, but to follow an old one. Venturing forth independently means having to repeat mistakes that could have been avoided, feeling frustration that might have been escaped. If there are standard ways of holding a guitar, or putting tension on the strings, the reason for this is not law, but effectiveness. These methods have been shown time and again to be useful for becoming a guitarist.

There is a spiritual lesson to learn from this. Is there only one way to pray, or to study the Bible, or to share the gospel? Of course not. However, there is a lot of wisdom that has accrued over millennia of experience regarding the basics of Christian discipleship. To try to figure out by oneself how to pray, or read the Bible, or practice the presence of God, or live in fellowship with other Christians, is not a mark of piety, but foolishness.

Returning to the illustration of painting a house one last time, in the end, I did finish the job. However, the workmanship was poor. (I know this because years later I repainted the house.) My ability to do the job well was restricted because I lacked the skills required. I fear the same is true for some Christian men. They are attempting to love their wives, to nurture the faith of their children, and to read their Bibles, but the effort is minimally productive. They have motivation; what they lack is competence. If their skills were developed, their efforts might bear more fruit. Further equipping might relieve frustration and multiply the harvest.

Vital Areas of Competence

We need to keep the goal of this book in mind. Our focus is on a baseline candidate, not a mature man of God. The agenda here is not to provide a comprehensive list of every potential skill that a Christian might develop, but to mention the core skills that a Christian dare not *not develop*. More can be built on this foundation. However, without this foundation further construction will be impeded.

Also, I need to specify that competence is not mastery, or even proficiency. If I am a competent carpenter, I have the minimum skill required to get a job done. There will be much I do not know. I know enough, not everything. There is a world of difference between a master and a journeyman. The goal here is to call guys to develop basic skills, not expertise. Any confusion on this point needs to be dispelled. If men think too much is being asked of them, they will feel despair, not motivation, and when it comes to the pursuit of godliness, men need all the motivation they can muster.

1 – Handling God's Word

A Christian unskilled in the Word is like an infantryman unskilled in weaponry. Next to Jesus Christ and the Holy Spirit, there is no greater gift that the Father has given us than the Holy Scriptures. They are food for the soul, a light for the feet, a scalpel for the heart, and a sword for defense. A man neglects them to his peril. The ability to 'rightly handle' (2 Tim. 2:15) the Word of God is more important in daily life than the ability to earn a living. A job connects us to money. The Scriptures connect us to God. It is no exaggeration to say that our spiritual wellbeing depends on meditating day and night on God's Word (c.f. Josh. 1:8, Ps. 1). In view of this, learning how to use the Bible is perhaps the most fundamental skill that a Christian can develop.

Dawson Trotman's classic illustration of the hand indicates what it means to be able to *hand*le the Word.[25] In the illustration, each finger represents a different way in which Christians need to interact with the Bible. The fingers are labeled 'memorize', 'study', 'read', and 'hear'. All of these activities are different. To know how to listen well to a sermon is different from knowing how to study the Word at home. The point to appreciate from this is that competency in the Word is not one thing. Just as being a competent soldier can be broken down into subsidiary skills—like leadership, weaponry, teamwork, orienteering, etc.—the same is true for handling the Word of God.

Perhaps the most brilliant aspect of Trotman's illustration is that he uses 'meditation' to label the thumb. What Trotman knew is that the key to having a firm grasp of the Scriptures is to internalize them through meditation. Without meditation we are grasping for truth without having the ability to hold onto it. In communicating this, Trotman was rehearsing the wisdom of generations of Christians. Only by attentively fixing our mind on the Word is the truth digested and the Spirit of Wisdom assimilated into our own being. Yet, if meditation is the end, memorizing, studying, reading,

---

25. The image is available online.

and hearing are the means. Without a thumb, grip is impossible, but without fingers, the thumb is of no use.

Every Christian man ought to aspire to fulfill Paul's counsel to Timothy: 'Do your best to present yourself to God as one approved, a worker who has no need to be ashamed, rightly handling the word of truth' (2 Tim. 2:15). This ability is a necessity, not a luxury. The Bible is unique in its power to make a man 'complete, equipped for every good work' (2 Tim. 3:17). Men ought to pursue this power with the vigor of beggars looking for food. With God's Word, men are strong. Without it, they are starved.

2 – Attunement to God through Prayer

Word and prayer are like inhaling and exhaling, two motions that complement one another. Of prayer and reading, one ancient writer says, 'When we pray it is we who speak with God, but when we read it is God who speaks with us.' Just as no person can inhale without exhaling, no Christian can read God's Word without desiring to speak to Him. Prayer is the most basic instinct of a newborn Christian, and a budding life of prayer is the most basic condition that signals when newborn Christians are beginning to grow.[26]

Prayer is a motion that contains different parts. There is adoration, confession, supplication, and thanksgiving.[27] Understanding the difference between each of these is important. Each part must be developed individually. There are a lot of men whose prayer lives are the spiritual equivalent to a weightlifting routine focused

---

26. For a brief exposition of this, read the simple, yet profound, hymn 'Prayer is the Soul's Sincere Desire' by James Montgomery.

27. A logical breakdown of all of the parts of prayer can be found in Isaac Watts, *A Guide to Prayer*. The text is available online.

entirely on chest and biceps. Often prayer is reduced simply to asking God for stuff (supplication) and saying 'thank you' for stuff given (thanksgiving). In fact, I would go further and say that a lot of men spend the whole of their Christian lives never figuring out what exactly adoration and confession are. Adoration is assumed to be the same as thanksgiving, and confession is more or less a polite 'I'm sorry' said in the presence of God.

This is tragic. Other than meditating on God's Word, I don't know of any spiritual practices that are more transformational than adoration and confession. To adore God—to profess the truth about Him regularly in prayer—is to experience the strings of the heart tightened back into a godly pitch of fear, wonder, gratitude, humility, dependence, trust, and availability.[28] Only through adoration does faith play in key. Confession is similar. The most powerful work of putting sin to death occurs on our knees. It is through confession that we come to diagnose the disease behind the symptoms, work up a spirit of godly sorrow that leads to repentance, and wait on the grace that alone can strike the root of our illness. Confession is far more than a polite apology; confession is mortification, the activity by which sin is put to death in the life of a believer. To be unskilled in such a vital practice is to allow a spiritual cancer to spread untreated.

Paul was not speaking to the spiritual elite when he said, 'Pray without ceasing' (1 Thess. 5:17). This is the calling of every Christian. Any man that would heed Paul's directive ought to begin by investing in the simple skills that make a life of prayer possible.

---

28. For more on tuning the heart through prayer see William Law, *A Serious Call to a Devout and Holy Life*, ch. 14. The text is online.

3 – Participating in Christian Fellowship

Paul repeatedly uses the metaphor of a body to indicate the way in which Christians are connected to Christ (the head) and one another (joint members). The edge of this image has grown dull due to overuse. Too many Christians think that being a 'member' of a church involves nothing more than attendance and tithing. However, Paul is not being fanciful in using the image. To be a Christian is to be vitally connected with other Christians, not just a narrow circle of 'spiritual friends', but a wide circle of men and women at various stages of faith. These relationships are not a necessary evil, but a precious good. Only by growing together does any Christian grow at all.

The idea of being competent in fellowship will be a foreign idea to a lot of men. To understand what I mean by this, fellowship needs to be thought about as a corporate experience and as a more personal experience. Corporately, Christians gather each week to do things that are special, unique, and *foreign* to everyday experience. The Word is preached, praise is sung, prayers are offered, and the sacraments are administered. A lot of guys enter into churches thinking that these activities are motions that can be performed without understanding. This can happen, but it is unhelpful. If men do not learn how to listen carefully to a sermon, how to connect heartily to the intercessory prayers of a pastor, or how to participate meaningfully in the Lord's Supper, these actions will feel perfunctory and meaningless.

Countless men skip church because they don't see the point. The long-term consequences of this are as devastating as indefinite fasting. Men need to be taught how to participate meaningfully in the public worship of God's people.[29] Men need to understand that the goal of gathered worship is not to dumb down the content but to train up the consumer. No parent mimics the eating habits of his or her children. At the table, children are slowly taught to eat like adults. Something similar should be happening to men as they partake in weekly worship services. They ought to cultivate an ability to benefit from activities, which, at first, seem foreign, even distasteful.

Yet, fellowship is also personal. Even more important than the structured worship of Sunday morning is the daily interaction that Christians have with one another. This interaction is unique and shaped by the truth of the gospel. Bonhoeffer notes, 'Christian community means community through and in Jesus Christ.'[30] This means that the code of 'niceness' and 'civility' inherited by secular culture is ill preparation for what it means to live together with other Christians. There are skills that go into maintaining Christian fellowship that are new and un-natural. Some examples of these skills are learning how to speak 'the truth in love' (Eph. 4:15), how gracefully to receive correction, how to acknowledge fault before another, and how to reconcile in the midst of conflict. Few men will have inherited a 'knack' for these things from their families and friends. Holding a grudge, clamming up, hiding sin, keeping a distance – this is the stuff that is second nature to men. Christian love is a new and awkward motion.

29.   James K. Smith is a useful guide for thinking about how participating in Christian worship is a holistic education. See James K. Smith, *Desiring the Kingdom: Worship, Worldview, and Cultural Formation* (Grand Rapids: Baker, 2009), part 2.

30.   Dietrich Bonhoeffer, *Life Together*, trans. John Doberstein (London: SCM, 1954), p. 13.

4 – Individual Stewardship

One of the rich legacies of the Reformation is the conviction that every Christian has a calling that he or she must fulfil. The idea comes straight from Paul who wrote: 'Let each person lead the life that the Lord has assigned to him, and to which God has called him' (1 Cor. 7:17). William Perkins, one of the earliest writers on the topic, says, 'If you would lead a life unblameable both before God and man, you must first of all think to yourself what your particular calling is, and then proceed to practice the duties of the moral law, and all other duties of Christianity in that very calling.'[31] The central idea of this was revolutionary 400 years ago and still is today. A man cannot pursue godliness who is unprepared to steward the life that God has given him.

What does this mean practically? It means that a man must know how to be faithful in the basic roles (husband, father, son, employee, etc.) and with the basic resources (time, intellect, money, property, family, etc.) that God has given him. No Christian owns the title deed to his life. Every one of us has been 'bought at a price' (1 Cor. 6:20). Thus each man must learn how to use his talents in order to honor the Lord Jesus Christ. For each area of life, be it finances, or parenting, or work ethic, the goal is to live in such a way that Christ will say, 'Well done, good and faithful servant' (Matt. 25:21).

Such stewardship will require a lot of schooling and *unschooling* for most men. To be a Christian husband bears only a faint resemblance to being a non-Christian husband. To manage finances in a worldly sense is a far cry from being generous in a

---

31. William Perkins, *Treatise of the Vocations.*

Christian sense. The indicators of being productive in the office are not the same as the indicators of redeeming time in the kingdom. In each major role, for each major area of responsibility, Christian men must be taught how to glorify God with the building blocks of life.

5 – Evangelism

The gospel is not a life-hack to be shared leisurely for interest and entertainment. The gospel is the power of God unto salvation for all who believe (Rom. 1:16). A final area where men need competence is in sharing the good news that Jesus is Lord.

Too many men feel inept at doing this. The root of the problem is sometimes confusion regarding what the gospel is. A man cannot share the gospel unless he is confident that he knows the gospel. In spite of recent criticism, one of the reasons that *The Four Spiritual Laws* and *The Bridge of Life* have been so effective for evangelism is because they are simple and everyday Christians have felt able to use them to share the good news. Men need to feel confident that they know the gospel and that the core message of the gospel is simple, relatable, and true. This confidence will go a long way to enabling ordinary guys to share in the Great Commission.

But there are two sides to evangelism. One is sharing the news of the gospel; the other is bearing testimony through a lifestyle that Jesus is Lord. Our charge is to be light in the darkness, to be sheep among wolves. If we conform to the world, we will not be able to testify that God's kingdom has erupted into the present age. Therefore, men must be taught not only how to share the gospel, but also how to resist the idolatrous practices that typify the world around them. Such resistance is more difficult than sometimes thought. It requires a prophetic eye, a tender conscience, and a courageous heart.[32] Men must be given the tools required to forge a distinctive Christian lifestyle, the ability to be in the world without being of it.

The Measurable of Competence

How does a man know when he attains competence as a Christian? The question is important because competence and self-confidence are easily confused. In truth, the two have nothing in common. Self-confidence is pride, the conviction that I can make progress in holiness apart from God. Jesus nips this attitude in the bud when He says, 'Apart from me you can do nothing' (John 15:5). *Nothing* – that is what the best of Christians can do on their own, now, always, *forever.*

If not confidence, what, then, indicates competence? The answer is disciple-making, the ability to pass on to others the basic form of life that has been given to me. In 2 Timothy 2:2 Paul says, 'What you have heard from me in the presence of many witnesses entrust to faithful men who will be able to teach others also.' This ability to teach what has been taught is the most important sign of competence. Who is a man able to pray? He is a man who is able to teach new Christians how to pray. Who is a man who can rightly handle the Word? He is a man who can instruct young believers in how to listen, study, and meditate on the Word. The ability to share in the task of making disciples, this is the key indicator of competence.

---

32. Jacques Ellul pinpoints the nature of the difficulty when he says, 'Christians ought to try to create a style of life which does not differentiate them from others, but yet permits them to escape from the stifling pressure of our present form of civilization.' See Jacques Ellul, *The Presence of the Kingdom*, Trans. Olive Wyon (Colorado Springs: Helmers and Howard, 1989), p. 46. For a beautiful example of what this looked like in the early church, see the second century text, 'The Epistle of Diognetus.' Translations of this text are available online.

Men Need Self-Control

⊲⊲⊲◆◆◆▷▷▷

M̲en like to pretend that they are warhorses. We tell ourselves
that self-control is a natural muscle that can be flexed at
will and that develops co-ordination and stamina over time. Our
problem with self-control, so we think, is not that we don't have it,
but that we choose not to use it. Like a warhorse, we are capable of
showing self-restraint in difficult circumstances. We are men, not
boys. We are soldiers, not recruits. So we think.

This is false. By nature we are not warhorses; we are mustangs.
A mustang has no capacity for self-control. It moves by instinct,
not discipline. A mustang behaves as all wild animals behave,
impulsively. No mustang could be taken straight from the wild
and placed in a battle. It would fret. It would flee. Ignoring bit and
bridle, it would not be able to control itself.

This is the condition of men outside of Christ. They cannot
restrain their basest appetites, much less direct their noblest faculties. The consequences of this are frightful. Spiritually, to pursue
godliness without self-control is like trying to swim with a millstone
tied around your neck. Intent does not matter. The strongest of
efforts is doomed for failure. But, thank God, Christians are not
in this condition. With the presence of the Spirit comes the power
for self-control. In Christ, men have no excuse not to develop this

grace-given virtue. Self-control is part of our inheritance in Christ (c.f. Gal. 5:22-23; 2 Pet. 1:6).

Avoiding Misunderstanding

When talking about self-control it is necessary to begin by clarifying what self-control is not. Not every brand of self-control is the same. There is true self-control, the fruit of the Spirit, and countless secular variants. Like counterfeit money, counterfeit virtues must be avoided.

First, self-control is not self-reliance. Self-control, like all of the fruit of the Spirit, is a product of grace. When we think about self-control we are mistaken if we imagine human willpower on steroids. Self-control is not a mental muscle that can be boosted artificially. Self-control is a complicated dance that only the Spirit-born are able *to begin* to perform.

Second, self-control is not self-mastery. Only God can see the depths of the human heart. Human motivation is every bit as complicated as the laws of quantum physics. No human being will ever achieve total mastery over himself. The motions of love, desire, fellowship, grace, and indwelling sin are too mysterious for this to happen. But if we cannot attain total mastery, we can attain a degree of control. The aim of self-control is for behavior to be deliberate, for truth to mold action, for the unconscious influences of an ungodly environment to be replaced with the spiritual influences of grace. Self-control has two opposites. One is being out-of-control. The emblem of this is a two-year-old. The other is being controlled by a godless environment. The emblem of this is a teenager.

Third, self-control is not absolute control. We are not princes sitting on thrones who can do as we please. God is sovereign; we are not. Our control is always limited to a station and calling ordained by God. Here the image of a warhorse is again helpful. A warhorse is under the authority of another. There is a lieutenant on its shoulders providing it with constant direction. Yet, a warhorse ought to have relative control. A good horse will not allow internal emotions or external circumstances to interfere with the lead of a rider. If all is done rightly, horse and rider are in sync. This is a picture of what self-control looks like for a Christian. Relative control, not absolute control, is what Christians are seeking.

So what is self-control? Self-control is the freedom and strength to follow a path to godliness, which is made possible through the working of the Holy Spirit. On the one hand, self-control is *freedom*. The human heart is not free by nature. It is shackled by sin, deluded by the world, and entrapped by Satan. This is why true, spiritual self-control (i.e. of the Holy Spirit) is impossible outside of Christ. If lust is resisted, greed sprouts to replace it.[33] The battle against sin is hopeless until sovereign grace is at work. On the other hand, self-control is *strength*. Self-control is the spiritual power to direct my steps according to the directives of God. He is the officer; I am the warhorse. Self-control is my ability to follow His lead.

I have met some Christian men who are uncomfortable with being told that they need to develop self-control. The reason is usually because the idea smells to them of 'legalism'. This reluctance is easily overcome. A single passage suffices to demonstrate the apostolic credentials of this virtue. In 1 Cor. 9:24-27, Paul says,

> Do you not know that in a race all the runners run, but only one receives the prize? So run that you may obtain it. *Every athlete*

---

33. For the true nature of killing sin see John Owen, *Of the Mortification of Sin in Believers*, ch. 5

exercises self-control in all things. They do it to receive a perishable wreath, but we an imperishable. So I do not run aimlessly; I do not box as one beating the air. But I discipline my body and keep it under control, lest after preaching to others I myself should be disqualified.

Paul's emphasis ought to be our emphasis.[34] His point is clear. No Christian should ogle at the disciplined lives of Lebron James, Serena Williams, or, for an older generation, Jerry Rice. The exemplars of self-control are Christians, not professional athletes. Our incentives are infinitely better than theirs. They are working for a perishable trophy. We are promised eternal life.

Why Men Need Self-Control

Without self-control there is conformity. Men need to understand this. Apart from grace, the laws of habit are as unavoidable as the laws of gravity. And how is habit formed? Rarely by intentional effort. Environment is the answer. Our natural preference is to steer using autopilot along a predetermined course. The problem is worse than laziness; it is blindness. Even where options are available to us, in most cases we fail to make a choice because we are blind to the alternatives. In the book *Mindless Eating* the authors estimate that on average there are 200 decisions regarding food every day that people do not make because they do not realize they are there.[35] What is true of eating applies with greater

---

34. In fact, Paul's insistence on self-control was so great that, when given the opportunity to speak about the Christian faith before the Roman governor Felix and his wife Drusilla, Paul reasoned about three things – 'righteousness and self-control and the coming judgment' (Acts 24:25).

35. Brian Wansink, *Mindless Eating: Why We Eat More Than We Think* (New York: Random House, 2006).

significance to the areas of parenting, lifestyle, work, marriage, leisure, discipleship, prayer, time management, and every other area of life. The Achilles heel of a lot of Christian men is not that they willfully desire to conform to the world around them, but that they never detach sufficiently to see where they are conforming and where they might be transformed. In this, they are like the Israelites in the Old Testament. The recurring idolatry in Israel did not happen because, like teenagers smoking pot, the Israelites were consciously trying to rebel against their divine parent. Idolatry happened because, like teenagers blending in among their peers, the Israelites unconsciously consented to common practices that *felt normal*. Self-control is the answer to mindless conformity. Only by getting a tight grip on the reins of life are we able to enjoy the freedom that God has given us in Christ.

Furthermore, self-control enables a man to avoid drift.[36] We all know what it is like to write down a list of priorities, such as having a quiet time or spending time away from work with the family, only to discover that over weeks, months, and years these priorities are forgotten and neglected. Demands at work have overshadowed responsibilities at home, or a lesser thing like fitness has displaced a greater thing like prayer. All of us are born like boats without an anchor. The currents of life carry us in unintended directions.

Yet, there is good news. With the gift of the Spirit comes not only an anchor, but a rudder, a wheel, and a map. The Christian need not drift; he can *steer*. In Christ, God has given him the kit required to follow the course of holiness. He can be anchored by

---

36. For more on drift see Michael Hyatt and Daniel Harkavy, *Living Forward* (Grand Rapids: BakerBooks, 2016), part 1.

principles; he can navigate by truth; he can steer with intent; he can resist the tide.

Moreover, self-control is vital for maintaining awareness of the living presence of God. There is no greater spiritual threat to men today than the gold rush to capture their attention. A Brave New World has been constructed to distract them incessantly with the trivia of news headlines, social media feeds, video games, and must-see entertainment. Not a second is left empty to meditate on Scripture or to contemplate the glory of Christ. As a result men are cut off from the feeding tube of grace. They are spiritually surviving on the rations of a death camp.

How can men avoid surrendering the gold of their attention? The answer is self-control. They can deliberately set their face to heed the apostolic counsel of Paul: 'Finally, brothers, whatever is true, whatever is honorable, whatever is just, whatever is pure, whatever is lovely, whatever is commendable, if there is any excellence, if there is anything worthy of praise, think about these things' (Phil. 4:8). These words are not good advice; these words are standing orders. Men must feed on the 'pure spiritual milk' of God's Word if they hope to 'grow up into salvation' (1 Pet. 2:2 ESV, NIV). But how can they do this? Only by means of self-control.[37]

---

37. Usually, when people think of self-control they think of resisting fleshly temptations. While this 'nay-saying' is not the only job of self-control, it is an important job of self-control. Self-control is indeed the ability to resist fleshly appetites in view of a greater good. But, in truth, the key to resisting these appetites is keeping the greater good in view. The more aware I am of God and delighting in His presence, the less attractive power temptation will have. Hence the importance of attention. Practicing the presence of God is the best tactic that a Christian has to neutralizing temptation in any given moment.

The Mechanics of Self-Control

It may seem unnecessary, even tedious, to break down the components of self-control. For this reason, I want to be clear why I am doing this. If men do not understand what self-control is, they will not be able to pursue it. Most people have a simplistic understanding of self-control. They reduce it to two basic motions. There is the brake pedal and the accelerator. To exercise self-control a person either presses down on the brakes to resist temptation (e.g. eating a second cookie) or steps on the accelerator to overcome fatigue (e.g. finish the last mile).

The truth is that self-control does indeed bear a resemblance to driving a car, but not in the way just mentioned. Regardless of what teenagers might think, driving is a complicated action. To drive well a person must use his imagination in order to think about different possibilities such as switching lanes, passing cars, and making turns. He must have clear and accurate vision in order to see what is happening around him. He must maintain concentration so as to avoid accidents and other unexpected perils. He must be decisive in critical moments, not allowing uncertainty or hesitancy to delay action. The simple motions of turning a wheel, flipping switches, and pressing pedals are, in truth, only a small part of what it takes to drive safely.

Self-control is similar. On the surface, self-control might look like two or three simple actions. However, a more careful look reveals that all of the faculties of the mind are at work enabling self-control to happen. Imagination, intellect, attention, memory, and the will all play a part. Understanding something about the role of each is important so that men can understand the task in front of them. The goal of self-control is far greater than resisting momentary temptations. The goal of self-control is to stay the course of holiness through a long and tumultuous life.

1 – The Role of the Imagination

If a man wants to control himself, he must be able to imagine the space of possibility before him. A high schooler will not consider enrolling in college unless he can first see himself as a college student. The potential of countless youth is restricted due to the shortsightedness of their imagination. They fail to aspire because they cannot see. If none of my parents, aunts or uncles, or grandparents received a college degree, I might assume that pennies on the hour is the best I will ever do. I will fail to attempt because I cannot imagine.

The spiritual application of this is important. Self-control requires a sufficient degree of detachment, reflection, and *dreaming*.[38] Human beings are always limited by the horizon of their vision. If I can only see 500 feet in front of me, then I will only operate based on that information. If I can only recognize the obvious options on the table, I will not factor further alternatives into my decision. This is why reading Christian biography is such a powerful activity. To read the life of Hudson Taylor is to reconsider what it might mean for me to depend on God. To pick up the story of William Carey is to reimagine what it means to live with a calling. The same is true for more commonplace decisions like how to disciple children, show hospitality, or manage finances.

---

38. Of course, there are dangers regarding dreaming. Paul Tripp says, 'But dreaming is never morally neutral because the dreamer is never neutral. Herein lies the danger of this intensely human gift. Our ability to dream is easily kidnapped by our sin. While our dreams can reveal our faith, they can also expose the lust, greed, selfishness, fear, anger, doubt, hopelessness, and materialism of our hearts.' Thus the challenge is dreaming according to what is true and holy, not what is false and sinful. Paul Tripp, *How People Change* (Greensboro: New Growth Press, 2008).

Most men follow the ruts of the people around them because they never pause to consider an alternative. They are not able to steer a different course into the future because their vision is limited to the lane right in front of them.[39]

2 – The Role of the Intellect

Every man views the world around him from a particular perspective. What I mean by perspective is the filter that spontaneously evaluates the options before me. For example, to see a packet of cigarettes is never just to see a packet of cigarettes. One man looks at some Marlboro Lights and thinks, 'A fun way to be cool'. Another recoils with the thought, 'A sure path to an oxygen tank'. For human beings, the world is never a cold assortment of scientific facts. We clothe everything we see with meaning and value. This is why being able to evaluate accurately is a vital condition of being able to choose well. If my perspective is wrong, my choices will be skewed. If I think earning a lot of money will provide me with a stable identity, then a long flow of decisions will be prompted by that evaluation.[40]

The point of this for us is that perception is more important than willpower when it comes to self-control. The will is a canal that typically follows the ridges dug out for it. In most cases, we *choose*

---

39. Along with books, life-on-life discipleship is another powerful way to adjust one's perspective on life. To observe how a mature Christian lives will generate new ideas regarding how to use time, raise children, manage finances, spend time with God, etc.

40. David Brooks says, 'Perceiving isn't just a transparent way of taking in. It is a thinking and skillful process. Seeing and evaluating are not two separate processes, they are linked and basically simultaneous…The person who has good character has taught herself, or been taught by those around her, to see situations in the right way.' David Brooks, *The Social Animal*, p. 127.

whatever we *value* most. The application of this is that, if we want to control our lives, we need to work hard to get a right perspective on what is true, good, and worthy of our aspiration. The mind must be detoxed of the false values of the world and reoriented by the truth revealed in Scripture. This is not easy work. Books must be read; the heart must be excavated; a worldview must be deconstructed; the seed of the Word must be sown in the heart so that a new perspective can take root. All of this is necessary labor. Only by attaining a true perspective can I begin to direct myself along the path of holiness.

3 – The Role of Attention

The relationship between where I focus my mind and how I direct my will is like the relationship between rain and the ocean. It is reciprocal. I can only exert self-control if I am faithful to fix my mind on what is true; I can only fix my mind on what is true if I exert self-control. There is no way of escaping this loop.

The reason attention is so important to self-control is because there is a drip feed from attention to what older theologians called the affections, those deep spiritual emotions like delight, desire, fear, hope, and sorrow. The more we *attend* to something, i.e. allow our attention to alight on it, the more our affections will nest on that thing. Any sports fan knows this. Every sports page, every episode of Sportscenter, every conversation about last night's game, is another dollar of love invested in sports. Practically, this explains why a lot of men cannot focus on God during prayer. They are not able to exert self-control because they have habituated their attention to attaching to other objects. There is a squatter's rights law that pertains to spirituality. Whatever we allow to sit on the mind will eventually have rights to the heart.

Therefore, a key front of the battle for self-control is to guard diligently the seat of the mind.[41]

4 – The Role of Memory

Genuine self-control is always the product of looking forward and looking back. No man will have the courage to follow the path of holiness unless he can *recollect* the faithfulness of God and *anticipate* (i.e. call to mind) the promises still to come. Self-control is something far more profound than a momentary flexing of a muscle. (Don't eat that cookie! Don't eat that cookie! *Don't eat that cookie!!!*) Self-control is the ability to follow a steady course through life, the ability to maintain a *character* within a vast, unfolding story. When we think of self-control we need to think of something more than decisions. We need to think of faithfulness, perseverance, and endurance. Self-control is for life what staying on track is for hiking. Self-control is the ability to avoid rabbit trails, subdue cowardice, and to overcome fatigue.

Human beings are narrating animals. We view our lives as if they are following a plot, and we instinctively attempt to reconcile the present moment with what has gone before and what, by faith, we take to be the end. One of the great challenges of being a Christian is that often the present looks irreconcilable with the end. Like Abraham, we see Isaac on the altar and cannot understand how God's promise will be made true. In such moments, memory

---

41. Thomas Watson says, 'The reason our affections are so cold to heavenly things is because we do not warm them at the fire of holy meditation. As the musing on amorous objects makes the fire of lust burn; the musing on injuries makes the fire of revenge burn; so meditating on the transcendent beauties of Christ, would make our love to Christ flame forth.' Watson, *The Christian Soldier*, part 4.

is vital for self-control. Memory reminds us of how God has led us thus far. We see the 'Ebenezer', the monument of help, and through this are strengthened to persist in the journey. Because of memory we don't need to act on feeling or mere human rationality. Reminded of who God is and what He has said, we are able to live by trust. We can steer by faith, not sight.

5 – The Role of the Will

The will does have a role to play in self-control. The best way to think of this role is not as that of a chief engineer or of a project manager, but that of a final inspector. In construction, an inspector does not build the house. His job is to make sure that the building has been completed according to code. The will performs a similar action with regard to our choices.

The job of the will is to place the stamp of *consent* on an action. Most of the work of making a choice or performing an action has already been done by the time the will gets involved. Nevertheless, this does not make the will unimportant. The will is that part of me that officially *approves* or *disapproves* a course of action. Once an action passes through the will I no longer have an excuse. I am now responsible. I signed the paperwork acknowledging that I was the one *willing* for a step to be taken.

There is an application of this that men need to consider. Consent can either be *active* or *passive*. I can pick up a rock and actively approve of the stoning of Steven, or I can, like Paul (then Saul), hold the garments of others and thereby give my passive consent. I can go out and build an altar to Baal like King Ahab and actively reject Yahweh, or I can follow the crowd to the high place and passively approve of the pagan ceremonies. Either way

I am guilty. Whether actively or passively, my approval stamped the proceedings.[42]

The relevance of this is as follows. A lot of men fail to honor God, not because they are actively, intentionally, and consciously choosing disobedience, but because through passiveness they are ignoring the leadership responsibility that God has given them. They unthinkingly adopt the habits of the world instead of testing these patterns by the Word of God (Rom. 12:2).

Men must be aware that they cannot shift the blame for their lifestyles. All of the time, whether actively or passively, they are giving their stamp of approval to actions, habits, and choices. Part of self-control is beginning to audit this consent and to search for areas of life where God is not currently being honored. Every man must examine himself to find both the areas where he is actively swimming against the agenda of God and also the areas where he is passively drifting in the current. There is no excuse for rubber-stamping ungodliness.[43] We must heed the counsel of Peter, 'As

---

42. In the useful treatise *The Improvement of the Mind*, Isaac Watts comments, 'For we are accountable to God, our Judge, for every part of our irregular and mistaken conduct, where He hath given us sufficient advantages to guard against those mistakes'. Men need to consider the extent of the guidance that God has given us through His Word. Our 'advantages' are great.

43. William Law's indictment regarding the spirituality of his generation needs to be repeated today: 'Let us judge ourselves honestly. Let us not vainly content ourselves with the common disorders of life: vanity of expenses, folly of diversions, idleness, wasting of time, thinking that these are unavoidable imperfections. Let us be assured that these imperfections are owing to this: we have not so much Christianity as to intend to please God in all the actions of our lives, as the best and happiest thing in the world. So we must not look upon ourselves in a state of common and pardonable imperfection, but in a state that lacks the first and most fundamental principle of Christianity: an

obedient children, do not be conformed to the passions of your former ignorance, but as he who called you is holy, you also be holy in all your conduct' (1 Pet. 1:14-15).

Men need to know that self-control is for the Christian Spirit-control. To exert self-control is nothing other than Christ living in us by means of the Holy Spirit (Gal. 2:20). It is this presence of Christ that transforms self-control from an impossible ideal to an actionable reality. Through Christ, and only through Christ, ordinary men can be more than conquerors (Rom. 8:37). We can be warhorses, not mustangs.

The Baseline Candidate

All of the pieces are on the table. We can now step back and see the outline of what a baseline candidate looks like.

First, he is a man whose heart has been captivated by a vision of divine glory. In the book *Back to Virtue*, Peter Kreeft rehearses a heart-check that Augustine first used centuries ago. It runs as follows:

> Imagine God coming to you and offering the following bargain: God offers to give you everything you can imagine in this world and the next as well. Nothing shall be impossible to you and nothing shall be forbidden. There will be no sin, no guilt. Anything you imagine can be yours. There is only one thing you will have to give up: you shall never see my face, says God (169).[44]

A captivated man is a man who shudders at this thought. For him, heaven is no heaven if God is not there. With David, he professes,

---

intention to please God in everything.' See William Law, *A Serious Call to a Devout and Holy Life*.

44. Peter Kreeft, *Back to Virtue* (San Francisco: Ignatius, 1992) p. 163.

'For a day in your courts is better than a thousand elsewhere. I would rather be a doorkeeper in the house of my God than dwell in the tents of wickedness' (Ps. 84:10). With Charles Welsey, he sings,

> *'Thy gifts, alone, cannot suffice*
> *Unless Thyself be given;*
> *Thy presence makes my paradise,*
> *And where Thou art is heaven.'*

Second, a baseline candidate has clarity. He understands that heaven and hell are at stake and that every trail through life leads ultimately to one place, the feet of Jesus. There will be much that this pilgrim does not understand regarding church doctrine, the Bible, and the world around him. Yet, he is confident in what he does know. He is thoroughly convinced that sin must be mortified, the devil resisted, temptation overcome, and the name of Christ honored. In addition, he is aware of the armor and provisions that God has given him for the journey. His mind is girded and ready for action (1 Pet. 1:13). For him, the world is a battlefield, not a playground. His spirit is watchful. His vision is focused. With George Whitefield he prays, 'God, give me a deep humility, a well-guided zeal, a burning love and a single eye – and then let men or devils do their worst!'

Third, he is not alone. He searches for spiritual friends like an injured soldier searches for a medic. He knows that the dangers of combat are too severe to hide alone in a foxhole. He needs other men in his life to guard his back, to edge him forward, and to support him in moments of fear, failure, and fatigue. He may not have a lot of these friends. There may only be a single Faithful, or Hopeful, to walk beside during some legs of the journey. But whenever possible, a baseline candidate avoids traveling without a comrade. He heeds the advice of Ecclesiastes, 'Two are better than one, because they have a good reward for their toil. For if they fall, one will lift up his fellow. But woe to him who is alone when he falls and has not another to lift him up!' (Eccles. 4:9-10).

Fourth, a baseline candidate is competent. He is not an ignorant recruit, sent out into the fire without the skillful knowledge needed to survive. He has been through basic training, and while there will always be more to learn, he has taken seriously Paul's exhortation to Timothy: 'Do your best to present yourself to God as one approved, a worker who does not need to be ashamed' (2 Tim. 2:15 NIV). His competence does not mean that he is always faithful. His best intentions often are left unfilled. But ignorance is no excuse for him. He is a man armed and able to serve 'the one who enlisted him' (2 Tim. 2:4).

Fifth, a baseline candidate is developing self-control. The world is a carnival of distraction to Christians. It offers no assistance in pursuing the things of God. Likewise, the heart is a cauldron of sinful passions, constantly bubbling forth with envy, covetousness, sloth, lust, and pride. How will a man maintain focus and direction as he follows the paths of righteousness? The answer is God's grace at work producing self-control. Without self-control, distraction and temptation will be an irresistible riptide pulling a man away from his intended course. With self-control, a man can resist the tide, and, by the power of the Holy Spirit, begin to navigate a course through life.

PART 3

The Plan

◁◁◁♦♦♦▷▷▷

The Way Forward

For many years I lived with my wife and children in Scotland. One of the 'joys' of being an expatriate was having to register the birth of a new child at the US consulate office in Edinburgh, a trip which, for us, took the best part of a day. The process began weeks in advance by booking an appointment slot online. These appointments were fixed and unchangeable. There was no mercy. To arrive a few minutes late did not result in a set of tender eyes acknowledging the difficulty of traveling with children and being allowed to squeeze into a later appointment. To miss the mark by an inch was to see the boat already launched on the horizon and to feel the despair of having to return all the way home in order to begin the process again, *online*.

I will never forget the fearful day when we went to register the birth of our fourth child, David. My preparations were impeccable and our departure on time. I left plenty of leeway just in case there were unforeseeable mishaps. Everything had gone fine until somehow—I still have no idea how it happened—I found myself completely lost in the middle of Edinburgh with inadequate navigation, no idea how to get to the consulate, and a clock tick, tick, *ticking*. Things went from bad to worse until, finally, the window to arrive on time closed to a paltry fifteen minutes. With only a penny of hope left, I pulled into a petrol station to ask once more for directions from a car beside me. Now Edinburgh is not Savannah, Georgia; it is not renowned for friendliness. In view of this, the man's reply astounded me. As if he were an angel sent from heaven, without fully understanding our predicament, he said, 'Follow me; I'll take you to the front door.' And so he did. Minutes later we were unpacked and standing at the entryway of the consulate, ready to endure the remaining ordeal of showing patient love to government employees.

I tell this story to reiterate the purpose of the third, and last, section of this book. My expectation is that most guys reading will feel a little bit like I did when I pulled into the petrol station in Edinburgh – frustrated, confused, and lost. In Edinburgh, I knew in theory where I needed to go. The difficulty was I didn't know how to get there from where I was. Most readers will be in a similar place if they have been following the trail thus far. Section one located where guys currently are. Section two identified where they need to be. The problem is that most guys are nowhere near this destination. In view of this, the final task is clear. The objective now is to bridge the gap, to offer guidance on how to get from A to B.

There is one additional idea I want to highlight from the story. Note what the man in Edinburgh did for me and what he did not do. He did take me to the front door of the consulate. This was tremendously helpful. But this was only stage one of a larger process. My family still had to undergo the rest of the procedure that eventually led to my son, David, being recognized as a US citizen.

I say this to reinforce the limits of this book. This book cannot certify men as mature disciples of Christ. No book can do this. At most, I can say, 'Come, follow me!' and point to a door. This front door is, in truth, the gate to a much longer road. Men must choose for themselves if they are willing to pass through this gate and continue further.

Now the aim of what follows is to be as concrete and practical as possible. I am a firm believer that ambiguity kills motivation. Too many men stall because they are uncertain what to do next. My hope is to help men pursue godliness by shining a light on any shadows. A clear itinerary is a priceless asset for any long and difficult journey.

What will be offered below are seven pieces of advice to help men advance toward the road to maturity. These steps are not pulled at random. Rather, they are the logical product of thinking about the problem and the solution as outlined thus far. None of these steps will be easy. Yet, men should not be disheartened by this. Prizes that are easily won are not worth keeping. Any heart trembling at the outset of this journey needs to meditate on Isaac Watts's hymn, 'Am I a Soldier of the Cross.'

> *Am I a soldier of the cross,*
> *A follow'r of the Lamb?*
> *And shall I fear to own His cause,*
> *Or blush to speak His name?*
>
> *Must I be carried to the skies*
> *On flow'ry beds of ease,*
> *While others fought to win the prize,*
> *And sailed through bloody seas?*

Are there no foes for me to face?
Must I not stem the flood?
Is this vile world a friend to grace,
To help me on to God?

Sure I must fight if I would reign;
Increase my courage, Lord;
I'll bear the toil, endure the pain,
Supported by Thy Word.

Catch a Better Vision of Glory

◁◁◁◆◆◆▷▷▷

M en, we need to view our admiration as a precious resource. There is an old fable of Aesop in which a miser melts all of his gold into a ball and buries it in the ground. Each day he digs it up only to stare at the hoard. One day a thief steals the gold. When the miser realizes that his prize is gone his spirits are shattered and he uncontrollably weeps. A neighbor, hearing the man's anguish, comes over and rebukes the man. The neighbor says, 'Did you ever intend to use the gold?' to which the miser responds, 'No.' Hearing this, the neighbor says, 'Then stare at your hole, for looking at a hole will do you just as much good as looking at a lump of gold.'

Like the miser in the fable, a lot of men do not appreciate the value of their ability to admire, and thus they waste a precious spiritual resource that needs to be invested wisely. Alain de Botton, a provocative writer, even if spiritually shortsighted, makes the following observation:

> The impulse to admire is an ineradicable and important feature of our psyches. Ignoring or condemning it won't kill it off; it will simply force it underground, where it will lurk untended and undeveloped, prone to latch on to inappropriate targets. Rather than try to

suppress our love of celebrity, we ought to channel it in optimally intelligent and fruitful directions.[1]

Christians ought to heed this advice. We need to realize that all of the time various celebrities are being marketed in an effort to capture our admiration. All around us there are apostles proclaiming the glory of athletic achievement, the glory of success, the glory of refined taste, the glory of extreme fitness, the glory of hedonistic pleasure. In truth, marketing is nothing more than a method of redirecting our admiration so that our lifestyle will change. Modern companies have absolute faith in Jesus' words: 'Where your treasure is, there your heart [and wallet] will be also.'

In this spiritually competitive environment step one to spiritual transformation is catching a vision of real glory. Until we love what is absolutely good, we will never have strength to pursue what is eternally holy. But how does a man go about doing this? Here are three suggestions.

First, listen to the writer of Hebrews and set your eyes on Jesus, the author and perfecter of faith (12:3). Jesus Christ is the splendor of holiness. The nearest we will ever get to tasting the fountainhead of all that is true, good, and beautiful is beholding the form of Christ. He is glory. Therefore, to see Him is to experience the very best, not just of earth, but of heaven. Recognizing this, the great Puritan John Owen writes, 'So if we desire strong faith and powerful love, which give us rest, peace and satisfaction, we must seek them by diligently beholding the glory of Christ by faith.'[2] This diligent beholding of Christ by faith is precisely what men must develop.

---

1. Alain de Botton, *The News: a User's Manual* (New York: Vintage, 2014).

2. John Owen, *The Glory of Christ* (Edinburgh: Banner of Truth, 2015), p. 7.

The blessings of doing this far outweigh the costs. In Jesus' first miracle at Cana the master of the feast, after tasting the miraculous wine created by Christ, calls the bridegroom and proclaims, 'You have kept the good wine until now.' Every heart that tastes and sees the goodness of God revealed in Christ says the same. Compared to the richness of love experienced in Jesus, the choicest of delights in this world are a diluted wine too dull and vinegary to be pursued with vigor.

Still, more clarity is required. How precisely does a man go about sustaining a vision of the glory of Christ? One way is outlined by J. I. Packer in the book *Keep in Step with the Spirit.* Packer advises a 'constant meditation on the four gospels, over and above the rest of our Bible readings.' In fact, Packer goes on to say, 'We should think, rather, of the theology of the epistles as preparing us to understand better the disciple relationship with Christ that is set forth in the gospels, and we should never let ourselves forget that the four gospels are, as has often and rightly been said, the most wonderful books on earth.'[3] The end of this quotation merits a pause for reflection. The gospels, says Packer, are *the most wonderful books on earth.* In fact, we can augment the statement. The gospels are more wonderful than any movies, any television shows, any music, any sports competitions, as well as any other books. If a man wants to behold the glory of Christ, he needs to meditate on the gospels, which is to say read them slowly, prayerfully, reverently, and submissively.

Another way is to meditate on select hymns and other New Testament passages that distill for us the beauty of who Christ

---

3. Packer, *Keeping in Step with the Spirit,* p. 71.

is and what He has done. Passages like Colossians 1:15-20, Philippians 2:5-11, and Revelation 1:12-18 are readily ignitable. The faintest spark of faith will turn them into a burning flame of devotion. Many of the classic hymns are similar. To pray through the hymns of Isaac Watts, Augustus Toplady, John and Charles Wesley, or even those of contemporary hymn writers like Stuart Townsend and the Gettys, is to see Christ through the eyes of a smitten heart.

Regarding hymns, my recommendation would be to begin with Isaac Watts's classic, 'When I Survey'. The wonder of this hymn is that it both presents a sublime portrait of the sacrificial love of Christ while also communicating the very mechanism by which beholding results in transformation. No hymn does a better job summarizing and revealing the power of the gospel than this one.[4]

Besides meditating on Christ, a man who is serious about catching a better vision of glory needs to think hard about the identity of God. Nothing hinders the spiritual development of men more than a small and distorted understanding of the Eternal. In *The Knowledge of the Holy* Tozer is absolutely correct when he says that the most important thing about a person is what comes to mind when they hear the word 'God'. Men must realize that God is the bedrock of everything else. Knowing Him matters more than any other kind of knowledge.

---

4. Any man who attempts to memorize this hymn needs to be careful not to miss the forgotten fourth stanza of the original composition:

> *His dying crimson, like a robe,*
> *Spreads o'er his body on the tree;*
> *Then I am dead to all the globe,*
> *And all the globe is dead to me.*

In order to improve this understanding, classic books like Packer's *Knowing God* and Tozer's *Knowledge of the Holy* are required reading for any serious Christian man. But be warned: such books are not tourist sites to be ticked off the list because they have been visited once. As C. S. Lewis remarks in his essay on reading great books, no one has truly read a great book if he has only read it once. Books like *Knowing God* are not meant to be perused like a newspaper but digested like food. When opening a book about God a man must realize that he is standing on holy ground. Even if he does not take off his shoes like Moses, the posture of his heart should be face down, humbly reverent before God. There is nothing wrong with reading a book of theology on your knees, combining study and prayer such that any new knowledge about God is burned on the altar of meditation, prayer, and praise.

Furthermore, to gain a better vision of glory men ought to seek a better vision of godliness. What is godliness but an incarnation of spiritual truth in the life of a particular man? To see a godly man is to view a moon, which, while not as bright and glorious as the sun itself, nonetheless reflects the same light in a different setting. Now there is no better way to change one's vision of godliness than by reading Christian biographies. In a thrilling lecture entitled 'The Greatest Fight in the World', Spurgeon says,

> When I read the lives of such men as Richard Baxter, David Brainerd, Robert Murray M'Cheyne, and many others, why, I feel like one who has bathed himself in some cool brook after having journeyed through a dark country which left him dusty and depressed. I feel this way because such men embodied Scripture in their lives and illustrated it in their experience...To see the effects of the

truth of God in the lives of holy men confirms faith and encourages holy aspiration.[5]

I have certainly found this to be true in my own life. To read the life of Dawson Trotman is to feel a passion surge to go out and train up disciple-makers. To spend a few days surveying George Mueller is to feel a painful longing to become a man of prayer and of trust. To track with George Whitefield or John Wesley is to feel convicted of wasted time and lost opportunity and to experience a creative spark igniting further passion to live and die for Christ. Typically, men who are bored by godliness are men who are ignorant of the godly. Those feeling their passion for God on the wane can do nothing more beneficial than taking up the life of a Christian hero and spending time in his, or her, company.

But what is true of the dead is also true of the living. Saints do not need to be dead in order to be admired. If a man is serious about improving his vision of godliness, living role models can be as useful—at times even better—than completed lives. The reason for this is that, whereas Christian biography is often a form of hagiography, highlighting strengths while ignoring weaknesses (and thus generating despair while inspiring fervor), in the living we see both the ore and the dross together.

Something is wrong if a man cannot answer the simple question, 'Who are your role models?' A man serious about growth will have a small circle of men, living and dead, who capture his imagination and who collectively represent for him the Christian he hopes to become.

---

5. The quote can be found in Spurgeon's final address to the Pastor's College, often published under the title, 'The Greatest Fight in the World'.

Clarify a True Perspective on Life

◁◁◁◆◆◆▷▷▷

True perspective is hard to come by. I recently saw an advertisement for the drink Crown Royal that ended with the slogan, 'Live generously and life will treat you royally'. Like all slogans, this one works because it picks up on an assumption that is already rooted in the hearts of a mass audience.[6] People today believe that life is supposed to be comfortable and relatively free of difficulties.[7] This is true among Christians and non-Christians. It is not as if we are unaware that sickness, tragedy, or failure might disrupt our plans. Yet, these 'evils' are viewed as irregularities. Just as we step into our cars each day expecting that they will take us to our destination without malfunctioning, we think that the normal conditions of life are health, prosperity, and success, unless, that is, we have bad luck and get a flat tire.[8]

---

6. Jacques Ellul explains the mechanics of this in *Propaganda: the Formation of Men's Attitudes* Trans. Konrad Kellen (New York: Vintage, 1973), pp. 6-57.

7. David Brooks's chapter on 'The Big Me' is an excellent diagnosis of this. See *The Road to Character*, ch. 10.

8. The sociologist Anthony Giddens describes how the modern world creates the feeling of a 'protective cocoon', buffering an individual from risk and danger. Anthony Giddens, *Modernity and Self-Identity: Self and Society in the Late Modern Age* (Cambridge: Polity Press, 1991), p. 136

Now my goal is not to make men into Puddleglums.[9] Neither pessimism nor optimism has anything to do with Christian hope. My aim, rather, is to make men sober-minded and alert (1 Pet. 1:13), so that they are not surprised when life feels more like a contest in the Colosseum than a stroll through a shopping mall.

What is the practical application of this? Once men have a foundational understanding of the gospel and the doctrines of grace, they then need to develop a true perspective on the nature of the Christian life as a whole. There is no better way of doing this than reading John Bunyan's classic, *Pilgrim's Progress*. In this allegory a man will find an itinerary that will outline the basic path that every Christian follows from conversion to death. Spurgeon allegedly read this book every year. In fact, he called *Pilgrim's Progress* 'the Bible in another form'. So it is: the substance of the Bible rewritten as the story of an individual Christian. In writing the book Bunyan did a miracle of cartography. He combined the lived experience of normal Christians with the unchanging truth of God's Word so that a road map of faith was published. Every Christian man needs a copy of this road map.

Second, I advise men to think hard about the triumvirate of evil that will contest their loyalty to Christ throughout their lives – the devil, sin, and the world. Nothing in our secular education will prepare us for spiritual combat. The devil is consigned to sit among the gorgons, dragons, and sea monsters of the past, a relic of a mythical age when adults were childish and human psychology misunderstood. Sin is another name for religious

---

9. Puddleglum is the unforgettable pessimist in C. S. Lewis's book, *The Silver Chair*.

taboos that do more to restrict happiness than promote any legitimate good. The world is a stage for self-promotion that will honor my desire for success so long as I am nice and tolerant of others. This is the underlying worldview of the world which will inevitably distort a man's life unless he is willing to grab a hammer and do some demolition.

For a right view of the devil and his cunning, a man can do no better than read Thomas Brooks's little book *Precious Remedies against Satan's Devices.*[10] One of the providential events that contributed to the Union army winning the Civil War occurred when a Union soldier found a detailed copy of Robert E. Lee's orders for the Antietam campaign on a cigar wrapper. An equally marvelous act of providence will occur if any man takes the time to read this book by Brooks. There he will read a full account of the strategy that Satan intends to use against him. If the reader heeds Brooks's advice, by God's grace, he will prove the truth of the Proverb, 'For in vain is a net spread in the sight of any bird' (1:17).

For sin, John Owen is an incomparable guide. His trilogy on indwelling sin, temptation, and mortification are like food, water, and shelter, the basic provision that every Christian requires to avoid sickness and death. Though Owen himself requires enormous patience and effort to read, thanks be to God, there are updated copies that translate his tortuous English into more accessible language.[11]

---

10. Along with Brooks a man would do well to read C. S. Lewis's classic, *The Screwtape Letters* (London: Collins, 1986).

11. A great starting point is Kris Lundgaard's book, *The Enemy Within: Straight Talk about the Power and Defeat of Sin* (Phillipsburg: P&R, 1998).

Third, for understanding the world, I would encourage men to take up another allegory, less known than Bunyan's, and perhaps slightly more difficult, called *The Labyrinth of the World and the Paradise of the Soul* by the great Czech reformer, John Amos Commenius.[12] The focus of the book is the journey of a man searching for his calling in life, who is led by a character named 'Delusion' to consider all of the various roles available to him, only to discover that his deepest needs are fulfilled only by Christ.

A final book that I would recommend that will teach men how to be on the offensive, not defensive, regarding their pilgrimage of faith is Thomas Watson's brief work *The Christian Soldier.* The focus of this book is what Watson calls 'holy violence', that is, a purposeful and vigilant self-exertion for the sake of holiness. From this book a man will glean a quick overview of the practices that contribute to spiritual growth. He will also correct the all too common evangelical assumption that grace and effort are opposed to one another.[13]

If this section feels like a reading list there is good reason for this. Gaining a better perspective on life requires thinking, and there is no better way to think well than by pondering the ideas of those who are remembered for their spiritual genius. Thinking is not the be all and end all of Christian living; however, for good reason Paul connects spiritual transformation with being 'renewed in mind' (Rom. 12:2). For many of us, such renewal will be painful

---

12. John Amos Commenius, *The Labyrinth of the World and the Paradise of the Heart*, Trans. Howard Louthan and Andrea Sterk (Mahwah: Paulist Press, 1998).

13. For example, Watson says, 'Our salvation cost Christ blood; it will cost us sweat.' Watson is filled with similar gems.

and burdensome since we live in a culture that associates leisure with turning off one's intellect. Such difficulties must be viewed for what they are, *weaknesses*, and overcome accordingly.

Furthermore, if the tone of this section feels morose we must keep two things in mind. The first is where we began. Step one is not pondering the evil of the world or the difficulty of life but rather the beauty of Christ. It is love and desire that fuel our race. We must remember this. But in addition, we must realize that the content of this section is determined by the deficiencies of the prevailing worldview within our culture and within our churches. There are pockets of Christianity where doom and gloom is preached every Sunday. But such places are like VHS players; hard to come by. Most Christians can go months, if not years, without hearing a plain sermon on the devil, the world, or indwelling sin. As a result a lot of believers have a lopsided diet. On the one hand, every song on Christian radio reminds them of the unfailing love of God and of His free grace toward sinners. On the other, core truths concerning the substance of spiritual combat are kept in the closet because they do little to attract a crowd. If my emphasis is imbalanced that is intentional; my goal is not to give a comprehensive perspective of Christian discipleship but to adjust the bass to match the treble.

Develop Competence in
the Fundamentals

◁◁◁◆◆◆▷▷▷

As a child I remember shooting hoops outside my grandmother's home. One of my uncles who knew a thing or two about basketball came up to me and asked me what I was working on. I told him that I was practicing a new move. It required dribbling the ball between my legs, doing a quick crossover behind my back, juking the defense with my eyes, then dribbling the ball back in front of me, only to conclude with a quick drive to the goal and score (crowds going wild, of course). It was a move designed for James Hardin, not for Joe Barnard. Nonetheless, I had seen a kid do something similar at the local YMCA and was committed to perfecting it. Fortunately, I had a gracious uncle. I remember him showing interest in the concept, but then gently encouraging me to start with something more basic because, so he told me, the simple is usually more effective than the fancy.

The simple is certainly more effective when it comes to spiritual things. Any Christian who learns the basics of prayer, meditation, and abiding in Christ—and consistently performs them—will find himself a man among boys. I remember asking a seventy-year-old man who was ripped for his age what the secret of his fitness was. His answer was that he was the guy who kept showing up.

Whereas others drift in and out of gyms over their life, more or less committed depending on the phase, he had never wavered in his workouts. For some reason the answer surprised me. I had hoped that there was something supernatural, genetic, or freakish regarding his strength. Anything extraordinary would have left me off the hook. The answer I did not want to hear was that the secret was persistence in the fundamentals. That answer closed the gap between me and him and left me uncomfortable, feeling like a decision stood before me that I could not ignore.

Ultimately, every man ought to strive to persist in the fundamentals of faith. However, for this to happen, something preliminary must occur first. He must develop basic competence. How can he do this?

The process begins by men realizing that they are players, not waterboys. There are some churches that treat men as if their job is to make sure the players in the game have everything they need to perform well. Thus men are asked incessantly to donate money, to volunteer to watch kids, to pray for those in 'fulltime ministry', and to ogle at the glorious anguish of a man on stage. When this happens men feel as if their contribution to the mission of God is minimal and, consequently, many lose spiritual drive. To fix this distorted mindset, men need to realize that they are players whom God wants on the field, using their gifts and opportunities to advance His kingdom. Appreciating this can radically change how a man views the importance of developing spiritual competence. The waterboy for the Los Angeles Lakers feels very little pressure to master the arts of dribbling, shooting, and passing. He knows he will never be called onto the floor. Every player on the bench feels differently. Each knows that he has a role to play, and that the performance of the team depends upon every team-mate, first to last, accepting and improving his abilities.[14]

Once a man feels the need to develop basic proficiency in the fundamental skills of discipleship he then needs to go and find training – not mere teaching, but training. This training does not need to be formal. If a man wants to learn how to pray, he does not need to wait until his church offers a course. All he needs to do is scour the local Christian community for a man who shines like a lighthouse as a model of prayer. Once he finds this model, he needs to ask the other man if he can track with him, that is, observe his prayer life, share prayer time together, and receive any further tips learned through time and experience. This same idea can be repeated for Bible study, parenting, meditation, evangelism, mentoring, and so on. The familiar aphorism that 'more is caught, than taught' is true. Hanging out with the right men will often be more effective than spending hours in a lecture hall.

A further piece of advice regarding competence is the need to match 'the practice zone' with 'the performance zone'.[15] Growing up I did not know any adults who were proficient musicians. What

---

14. The London Institute for Contemporary Christianity has a lot of useful material to help Christians appreciate the importance of everyday life in the mission of God. A good place to begin is their DVD course, *Life on the Frontlines*.

15. Dawson Trotman, whose knack for discipleship was uncanny, says, 'We all need that extra push and the challenge of something to aim for to get us to do what we know we ought to do but can't do on our own.' Skinner, *Daws*, p. 153. There have been plenty of books written in recent years on the concepts of 'deliberate practice' and 'the practice zone'. For an introduction to these concepts see Daniel Coyle, *The Talent Code* (New York: Bantam Books, 2009) and Eduardo Briceno's TED talk, 'How to Get Better at the Things You Care about'.

I did know was a lot of men who had learned a few classic rock songs in high school and college and who periodically got the guitar out of the case in order to run through the same, tired repertoire. It struck me early on that in music, or fitness, or Bible knowledge, most people plateau early. They reach a limited ability which then defines their performance for the remainder of their lives.

Why this is true is not difficult to understand. People prefer comfort to strain, pleasure to pain. As a result, we seldom challenge ourselves to exceed what we are comfortable with. This is why athletes need coaches and musicians need teachers. Rare is the person who, left to his own devices, will challenge himself to grow continually and to resist a state of equilibrium.

This place of developing new skills and being challenged to exceed current abilities is 'the practice zone'. If a man is serious about growth, it is important that he periodically joins groups or finds spiritual coaches that press him into the space of discomfort, difficulty, and struggle. Jesus repeatedly did this to the twelve, at times asking them to do what looked impossible or sending them out on missions that they never would have dared attempt on their own. Men need to find mentors and spiritual directors who will do the same. The activity might be as simple as reading a book; it might be as scary as sharing the gospel with a neighbor. The possibilities are endless. The point is that inertia will set in for any man unless periodically some outside force disrupts the status quo. Just as there are thousands of guitarists who are no more proficient at sixty than they were at twenty, there are countless Christians whose competence in spiritual things remains unchanged after a few formative years on the backside of conversion. Men, don't let this happen to you.

Band Together with Like-Minded Men

◁◁◁◆◆◆▷▷▷

In *Men against Fire* Marshall made an observation that merits spiritual application. Marshall noted that men fought best when grouped in what he called 'fire-teams'. These teams were small groups of four to six soldiers who were ordinarily grouped around a natural fighter. The benefits of this structure were both pragmatic and psychological. Pragmatically, soldiers guarded each other's backs. Psychologically, the morale of each man was boosted because he was not just fighting for his own survival, but for the survival of the group.

Christian men ought to consider the truth of Marshall's analysis. One of the greatest risks a man can take is to attempt the Christian life on his own. The deceitfulness of the heart by itself is a sufficient reason to walk close to others who are wise and faithful. Long ago Solomon recorded the proverb, 'Whoever isolates himself seeks his own desire; he breaks out against all sound judgment' (Prov. 18:1). This wisdom is much needed today. A man who isolates himself is a man in danger.

How does a man go about building a spiritual fire-team? The first step is being on the lookout for other men who have similar passion and direction in life. Not every Christian will be a candidate for spiritual friendship. There will be some Christians whom we are called to love, not befriend. There will be others whom we are called to disciple, but who never reach the trust level required to adopt as spiritual friends. To have different circles of intimacy is not a sign of sinfulness, but a fact of life in a fallen age. To limit spiritual friendship is not to build a wall that restricts self-involvement, but to build a door to make sure that at least a few select individuals have access to the underlying 'me'.[16]

Step two is to test these friendships by being more open about spiritual things: to share more about myself, to talk about the joys and difficulties of following Jesus, and to see whether personalities 'click' in such a way that seals a relationship.[17] The sign of a true spiritual friend is fellowship in Christ and with Christ. This sharing of Jesus together is what more than anything else distinguishes spiritual friendship from any other kind. If a friend inspires a sweeter delight in Christ, a deeper desire to know Him better, a firmer hope that he is faithful, and a quicker fear of anything that smells of sin, a spiritual friendship is taking root.

The third step is acknowledging the intent of the friendship. This need not be formal. Yet, formality is not always a bad thing. Stephen Mansfield has a useful section on what he calls 'the covenant transition'. He suggests a moment when two or more guys make explicit what was perhaps already implicit – that this friendship serves a higher purpose than mutual enjoyment. Most bands of

---

16.   Aelred notes that in heaven these limitations will be removed because, without sin, everyone will be able to trust everyone absolutely.

17.   This 'clicking' is not unimportant. Spiritual friendship cannot be forced. John Wesley understood this, which is why Methodist 'bands' were the only circle of Methodist fellowship that required the consent of all participants to admit a new member. See D. Michael Henderson's *John Wesley's Class Meeting: a Model for Making Disciples* (Wilmore: Evangelical Publishing House, 1997).

spiritual friends will benefit from having an open conversation like this. Such forthrightness gives men the opportunity to establish what Mansfield elsewhere calls a 'free-fire zone'. A group of guys can be clear that, within this circle, anything that must be said, *will be said.*

The fourth and final step is training together. For this, John Wesley is a useful guide. When it comes to combining vision and practice, few have excelled Wesley. What Wesley managed to do was provide his followers with both a sweeping vision of holiness and a structure of discipleship that targeted head, heart, and hands.[18] At the very center of this plan was small groups of four to six like-minded Christians meeting in what Wesley called a 'band'. A band was not a social gathering. It was a spiritual fire-team in which men stayed in regular communication regarding temptations and other spiritual struggles.[19]

One of the problems I see among churches today is that Christian leaders are promoting friendship rather than spiritual friendship. There is nothing wrong with having friends and hanging out. Nonetheless, a lot of Christian guys have friends already. What they lack is a spiritual band of brothers who will press them to stay focused on the way to holiness. Such spiritual camaraderie was one of the secrets of the early Navigator's movement. To hang out among Navigators in the 1940s was to feel a holy peer-pressure

---

18.   Ibid, p. 110ff.

19.   During band meetings, each member had to answer the following questions: 1. What known sins have you committed since our last meeting? 2. What temptations have you met with? 3. How were you delivered? 4. What have you thought, said, or done, of which you doubt whether it be sin or not? 5. Have you nothing you desire to keep secret?

to memorize Scripture, to study the Bible, to evangelize the lost, and to have a 'no-tolerance' attitude to sin. Navigators were not just friends who happened to be Christians. They were Christians bound together by spiritual friendship. Men need something similar today.

There is no end to the possibilities of how a band of guys might train together. My advice, however, would be to match doing with thinking, taking risks with drinking coffee. There is a gigantic world of need right at the feet of Christian men. No band of brothers can meet together for long without eventually having some daredevil ideas about how to turn the world upside down for Christ.[20]

20. The early Moravian fellowship under Count Zinzendorf provides a fascinating example of how close spiritual fellowship can lead to radical mission. See Phil Anderson, *The Lord of the Ring: In Search of Count Zinzendorf* (Minneapolis: Bethany House: 2007).

Strengthen the Muscles that Enable Self-Control

◁◁◁◆◆◆▷▷▷

Self-control, as I have described it, is not so much 'will-power' as the authority and freedom under Christ to work out our salvation with fear and trembling. In Christ, we are liberated, equipped, and authorized to take leadership for our lives and to direct ourselves and our families along courses that bring praise and glory to His name.

Understood in this way, self-control is less the action of a powerlifter performing simple motions via brute strength than the finesse of a wrestler whose actions depend upon multiple areas of fitness—flexibility, strength, co-ordination, and speed—all syncing together in support of a single, concerted effort. Therefore, the key to developing self-control is neither self-denial nor self-exertion, but rather an intentional cultivation of underlying 'spiritual muscle groups' such as the imagination, intellect, affections, memory, and will. Only when each of these are properly tuned is a man truly free to direct his steps along the path to holiness.

How does a man begin to do this? The key to freeing up the imagination is to engage in a sanctified version of life planning. A man who ignores the future is like a person who walks around staring at his feet. He will miss a lot of useful paths in life because he never looked up to survey the landscape. The undeniable benefit of life planning is that the activity protects a person from 'drift', the mindless persistence along an unspecified course. Of course, for Christians, a deep attitude of humility must correspond to any attempt at life planning, since our lives are ultimately in God's hands and because the future belongs to Him, not us. Nonetheless, most men will find spiritual relevance in Eisenhower's quip, 'Plans are worthless, but planning is everything'.

A useful guide to life planning is Michael Hyatt's book *Living Forward*. [21] Hyatt goes through all the nuts and bolts of the activity in a way that is simple and practical. However, Christians who read this book need to be cautious on two points. The first is that there is a secular assumption at the heart of not just this book but almost all of modern life planning that needs to be exposed as a lie. *This assumption is that the universe revolves around me.* Any Christian intending to think seriously about his future needs to begin with the most fundamental fact of all: everything, including me, exists for the glory of God.[22] Therefore, the goal of life planning can never, for the Christian, be happiness (as defined by psychology), self-fulfillment (as defined by pop culture), or success (as defined by me). The goal of life planning is good stewardship – figuring out how I can best use my gifts and opportunities to bring acclaim to the Triune God.

The second point of caution regards Hyatt's recommendation that a person write his eulogy. The logic behind the activity makes perfect

---

21. Michael Hyatt and Daniel Harkavy, *Living Forward* (Grand Rapids: BakerBooks, 2016).

22. Anyone needing to detox from the navel-gazing of the modern world should read Jonathan Edward's classic treatise *The End for Which God Created the World*.

sense. Men undoubtedly need to detach from the present and to get a long-term perspective on what they value and who they want to be. The problem is the point of view that Hyatt recommends. Looking back on life from the perspective of a eulogy inspires sentimentality, nostalgia, and a focus on temporary goods. For Christians, a better perspective to adopt is that of standing before the judgment seat of Christ. The question men need to face directly is not, 'What do I want for my life?' but 'What does Jesus want from me?' I may want for myself more comfort, more fun, and more 'me time'. Christ may want from me more sacrifice, more service, and more 'us time'.[23] Therefore, my suggestion to men is that, instead of writing their eulogy, they write a description of the life that Jesus desires them to live. If taken seriously, the result of this activity will be nothing less than a personal vocation, a clearer sense of that unique role that Jesus has summoned me forth from the dust to play.[24]

In terms of the intellect, we have already discussed the need for men to develop something akin to a Christian worldview. Yet, the emphasis before was on clarifying the nature of Christian

23.   This perspective ought to create a sense of urgency regarding how we use time. J. Oswald Sanders says, 'Suppose that we allot ourselves a generous eight hours a day for sleep (and few need more than that), three hours for meals and conversation, ten hours for work and travel. Still we have thirty-five hours each week to fill. What happens to them? How are they invested? A person's entire contribution to the kingdom of God may turn on how those hours are used. Certainly those hours determine whether life is commonplace or extraordinary.' Sanders, *Spiritual Leadership.*

24.   A useful guide to thinking about vocation is Os Guiness's book, *The Call: Finding and Fulfilling the Central Purpose of Your Life* (Nashville: Thomas Nelson, 2003). Equally fruitful will be meditating on some classic hymns such as 'Servant of All, to Toil for Man' and 'Forth in Thy Name' by Charles Wesley and 'Go Labor On' by Horatius Bonar.

discipleship. Here we need to touch upon a different aspect of a Christian worldview, namely, the need to understand the times in which we live. In one sense, there is nothing new under the sun. The struggle to be holy today is the same as the struggle 2,000 years ago. Yet, in another sense, holding an iPhone connected to an Instagram account does indeed distinguish my experience of the world from that of my grandfather. The calling of Jesus is unchanged: 'Be wise as serpents and innocent as doves'. But the application of this calling looks different depending on whether you live under an oppressive Islamic regime or whether you live under an oppressive materialistic regime.

Thus no man will be able to live responsibly before God unless he has some understanding of the specific nature of the spiritual combat around him. To fight a war against Al Qaida in Afghanistan is different from facing jungle militia in Vietnam. Likewise, to be faithful within the easy religion of the American Bible-belt is different from being faithful in the callous secularity of Scotland.

How does a man develop this understanding? There are two ways. The first is to read non-devotional books written by great Christian thinkers. There is a reason why people used to pay good money to get a 'liberal education' (liberal being taken in the sense of liberty). A prerequisite of freedom is having the basic knowledge of the truth and the robust faculties of mind required to make wise choices. There are no shortcuts for this. Christian men will have to think hard in order to be able to avoid the snares of the culture around them. Reading a collection of essays by C. S. Lewis or a book by Neil Postman will go a long way to transforming a man's understanding of the world.

The second way to develop a contemporary Christian world-view is by listening to 'prophetic' preaching. Let me be clear what I mean by this. The primary role of the prophet in ancient Israel was not to foretell the future but to highlight the invisible sin that God's people could not see. For this reason, Micah says, 'I am filled with power, with the Spirit of the LORD, and with justice and might, to declare to Jacob his transgression and to Israel his sin' (3:8). Similarly, in Lamentations we read, 'Your prophets have seen for you false and deceptive visions; they have not exposed your iniquity to restore your fortunes' (2:14).[25] If Christian men want to avoid following the ruts of the world, they need to find expositors of the Word who are able, as John Stott describes, to build bridges between the eternal truth of God and the mutable world around us. Such preachers do not need to be living. The prescience of a great preacher like Martin Lloyd Jones means that his sermons still speak even while he is dead.

What, then, about the *affections*? We must remember the inseverable connection between our attention and our deep spiritual emotions. There is a drip feed from one to the other. To sit in a football stadium and join in the crowd is to water an underlying passion for sports. To walk through a shopping mall is to feed a desire to consume. To read a newspaper is to rev up concern for current events. To meditate on Scripture is to kindle a love for God. The point here is not to say that men ought to become

---

25. This notion of prophets revealing sin is evident in the New Testament as well. Writing to the Corinthian church, Paul says, 'But if all prophesy, and an unbeliever or outsider enters, he is convicted by all, he is called to account by all, the secrets of his heart are disclosed, and so, falling on his face, he will worship God and declare that God is really among you' (1 Cor. 14:24-25).

monks and devote themselves exclusively to spiritual activities without interruption. (Not even monks do this!) The point, rather, is to convince men that they need to audit their attention and to make sure that the greatest goods receive the most attention. If a man spends ten hours a week watching sports and one hour a week engaging the Word, he needs to second guess his choices. His ability to serve Christ will be compromised because, over time, sports will become his first love. Proverbs warns us, 'Keep your heart with all vigilance, for from it flows the springs of life' (4:23). This injunction should not be ignored. Satan enjoys nothing more than reducing the reservoir of a Christian's love for Jesus by piercing a leak in the heart that looks insignificant. Fifteen minutes wasted here, thirty minutes squandered there, what difference does it make? Do the math over a lifetime and the results are devastating.

There is no myth more dangerous today than the belief that our time and our attention are spare change to be wasted on trivium. The heart is at stake, and the only way to guard the heart is by attending to the practices that maintain a spirit of devotion.

For any man looking for a simple and practical way to reinvest his attention, I would recommend the Topical Memory System produced by the Navigators. This system was devised by ordinary laymen to help guys learn how to incorporate meditation into their daily routines. The book that goes with the system gives an overview of how to memorize and meditate on the Word. In addition, by the time this memory course is completed a man will have already experienced the power and joy that come from storing God's Word in the heart.

Finally, I will say something regarding the *memory*. The connection between memory and hope has already been made. What we need to do now is to indicate how memory can be improved so that faith and hope are strengthened. The key for this is in the words of Hudson Taylor: 'We do not need great faith, but faith in a great God.' The bigger our conception of God, the stronger our faith and hope will be.

Here are two suggestions for how men can fortify their trust in God. The first is to spend some time with George Mueller. Mueller's remarkable life of building orphanages and keeping rigorous accounts of specific and supernatural answers to prayers is well known. Too often overlooked, however, is the daring mission that drove Mueller's life. Mueller's overarching intent was to provide public proof that the God of the Bible was as real, active, and available in the contemporary world as in the Sinai desert.[26] Behind each plea for another day's bread to feed orphans was the following audacious hope: that God would irrefutably demonstrate His faithfulness to a new generation of Christians. So He did, as the autobiography of Mueller gives plain evidence.

I have found that hanging out with George Mueller does two things for me. First, he increases my trust in the ever-present faithfulness of God. God stops feeling like a concept I *believe in* and becomes a living person who I am called to *partner with*. Second, Mueller sparks a desire in me to prove God's faithfulness in my own experience. I don't just want to read stories of what God has done for others; I long to have a testimony for myself of how the living God has cared for me.

---

26. Mueller writes, 'I also particularly longed to be used by God in getting the dear orphans trained up in the fear of God; but still, the first and primary object of the work was, and still is, that God might be magnified by the fact that the orphans under my care are provided with all they need, only *by prayer and faith,* without any one being asked by me or my fellow-laborers, whereby it may be seen that God is FAITHFUL STILL, and HEARS PRAYER STILL.' George Mueller, *Autobiography of George Mueller: the Life of Trust* ed. H. Lincoln Wayland (Grand Rapids: Baker Books, 1981) p. 115.

This leads to a second way to reinforce memory.[27] Risk obedience. Often when I talk to men I get the impression that they already know what God wants them to do. They just lack the courage to do it. If men want to strengthen their trust in God, they need to step regularly into the space of deeper faith and daring obedience. God wants to be God in the life of every believer. He will protect us, provide for us, and empower us if we abide in Him. If we are not experiencing the truth of this, the reason might be because we are attempting to manage life without God.[28] Only by being dependent upon the living God do we get to see His faithfulness in action. *Men, risk obedience.* The result will be a memory that testifies to the heart, 'Trust God more!'

---

27.   Memory here has a covenantal meaning such as found in Deuteronomy 8:18, 'Remember the Lord, your God.' Within a covenant, *to remember* is not so much to bring something to mind as to act according to a binding relationship.

28.   Os Guinness says, 'At its heart, the modern world is a decisive challenge to the authority of God outside our private lives. This is true not because a few atheists trumpet that "God is dead" but because our entire culture, Christians included, so relies on the gifts of the modern world that we have "no need of God" in practice.' *The Call*, p. 102.

Simplify Life

◁ ◁ ◁ ♦ ♦ ♦ ▷ ▷ ▷

Busyness is a badge of self-righteousness in the secular world. Just as Pharisees took pleasure in making their phylacteries wide and their tassels long, men today inwardly rejoice to complain to others how busy they are. We think busyness demonstrates an admirable work ethic, an ability to multitask, and a sense of achievement. In truth, busyness signals nothing more for most than conformity to the world's demands, the absence of self-determined priorities, and a lack of self-control. John Wesley famously said, 'Though I am always in haste, I am never in a hurry'. Every Christian man ought to aspire to be able to say the same. Any busyness that hinders our availability to God ought to be treated like a baited hook. There are no kudos among the angels for having been busy. God does not care that we live up to the expectations of the neighbors around us. What matters is that, like Jesus, at the end of life we can say, 'I glorified you on earth, having accomplished the work that you have me to do.'

How does a man go about this? The key is to simplify life on two fronts. First, cut the fat of ordinary life. More can always be added; however, to miss the most important due to the less important is tomfoolery. If a family needs more time to make sure that worship and discipleship are happening in the home, then do the obvious – say 'no' to the non-compulsory stuff of life. A child can rejoin a sports league twelve months down the road. Yet, the time lost in putting the things of God into his heart (Deut. 6) can never be recovered. Likewise, if there seems to be no time in the day for prayer and meditation, do a quick assessment of where time is being drained. Be radical. Give up watching College Football for a year; skip a deer hunting season; replace normal workout time with Bible study. Don't *not* develop the routine habits that, over time, promote spiritual maturity. Minor tweaking rarely fills the gap. Be willing to do an about-face. A lot of guys are stuck as spiritual infants because they lack the fortitude to repent. *Be a man.* Do what is needed to pursue God.

The other front requiring simplicity is a man's devotional life. Complexity kills habit. Simple and effective, these are the essential traits of repeatable action. The genius of Dawson Trotman was to produce what his biographer calls 'spiritual technology'. Just as a pair of clippers simplifies the act of cutting a hedge, having a method of Bible study, or prayer, does the same for a time of devotion. There is no need to reinvent the wheel. The wheel is a concept that, once invented, ought to be reproduced a million times. Therefore a wise man will scour the lives of other Christians looking for helpful tools to improve his spirituality.

But there is a further aspect of Trotman's legacy worth mentioning. For Trotman, simple never meant easy. This is where modern Bible studies so often go wrong. To remove the work involved in study is to remove the benefits accrued from study. One reason why Trotman was such an effective discipler of men was because he required that the men he discipled exert themselves. The technique was simple, but the work was hard. Passages had to be summarized, words had to be defined, cross references had to be looked up, and verses had to be memorized. Men need simple devotional lives, but men also need fruitful devotional lives. Be sure that what you do is simple and effective.

The Checklist

◁◁◁◆◆◆▷▷▷

Men are easily spooked. We are like calves, not bulls. If you give a man too many things to do at once, he will run and hide. In light of this, the worse way to end this book would be to leave men feeling overwhelmed by an impossible task. For men to succeed, the road needs to be made as simple as possible. Guys need a series of attainable action steps that will give them an immediate sense of momentum and direction. Therefore, in view of all that has been said in this book, here are eight actions that can immediately direct a man who is hungering for spiritual growth.

1 – Realize that On Your Own You Can Do Nothing

How did Jesus begin the Sermon on the Mount? He began with the statement, 'Blessed are the poor in spirit, for theirs is the kingdom of God'. The first step of any spiritual growth is realizing that we can accomplish nothing on our own. We are as dependent on divine grace for spiritual life as we are dependent on oxygen for bodily life.

2 – Memorize the Hymn 'When I Survey'

Only the Holy Spirit can ignite a blazing heart for Christ. However, what we can do is stack kindling on the grate, put newspaper beneath, and prayerfully wait for the Holy Spirit to strike a match. 'When I Survey' is what people in the Deep South call fat pine. The hymn is filled with flammable sap that readily ignites. My advice is to memorize this hymn, to meditate on it, and to pray through it. See if the Spirit doesn't use these stanzas to stoke the embers of the heart into a fire of devotion for Christ.

3 – Read Pilgrim's Progress

A lot of books have been mentioned in this chapter. Begin by reading *Pilgrim's Progress*. There are updated versions, rewritten in contemporary English.[29] Find one that works for you and watch as Bunyan's spiritual classic becomes an itinerary for life. In addition, if you have children, purchase the illustrated and abridged version *A Dangerous Journey*. The illustrations will help children and adults alike appreciate that joyful trepidation that comes with following Jesus.

4 – Find Two Spiritual Friends: One Living, One Dead

There is no reason to restrict friendship to contemporaries. After you go and find a living spiritual friend, then take up a biography and begin the process of getting to know someone who has completed life and is now in glory. One of the best pieces of advice I ever received was to make a list of my 'big five'. I was told to pick five people from history and to make them into an intimate circle of acquaintances. They didn't have to be preachers or missionaries. They could come from any background or vocation. The idea was to undergo the kind of study that Plutarch performed when writing his famous *Lives* of imminent Greeks and the Romans. In a well-known passage, Plutarch says,

> I treat [each life] as a kind of mirror and try to find a way to arrange
> my life and assimilate it to the virtues of my subjects. The experi-

---

29. One modernized version is John Bunyan, *The Pilgrim's Progress in Modern English*, ed. L. Edward Hazelbaker (Newberry: Bridge Logos, 1998).

ence is like nothing so much as spending time in their company and living with them. I receive and welcome each of them in turn as my guest…and choose from his achievements those which it is particularly important and valuable for me to know.[30]

My recommendation to men is to start by just choosing one life to study. Read about Robert Murray M'Cheyne, Dawson Trotman, Hudson Taylor, Charles Spurgeon, Jim Elliot, or Dietrich Bonhoeffer. If it is true that a man is the average of his five closest friends, you will only benefit from adding at least one Christian hero to your most intimate circle of brothers.

5 – Complete the Topical Memory System

I know a lot of older men who have devoted time to memorizing and meditating on Scripture. I know very few young men who have done so. Meditation has never been a common practice among Christians; however, it appears increasingly to be a dying art. I know of nothing more transformative than meditation and adoration, but like Latin and Greek, neither skill is taught today.

The easiest way to begin to meditate is to memorize. The Topical Memory System has been used by thousands of Christians with continued blessing. Regardless of how old you are, or how dilapidated your memory is, do not neglect the call of Psalm 1 to meditate on God's Word day and night.

6 – Read a Christian Book on Modern Culture

In *The Time Machine* the time traveler ends up in a bizarre future age where the planet is populated by two strange creatures. The

---

30. Plutarch, *Roman Lives*, trans. Robin Waterfield (Oxford: Oxford University Press, 1999), p. 42.

Eloi are a kind of domesticated human being that pursue childish play while trying to forget the fact that they are farmed as food. The Morlocks are a subterranean creature that only venture forth at night in search of prey. Christians need to be careful to avoid the naivety of the Eloi. The world will feast on us—our time, our money, our children, our work, our leisure—unless we are informed and watchful.

Most guys are not readers when they become Christians. However, Christianity is a magical force that tends to transform class clowns into budding intellectuals. My suggestion is to begin this process by reading Neil Postman's book *Amusing Ourselves to Death*. Although the book is slightly dated, Postman (who is now deceased) had a gift for taking difficult cultural analysis and making it plain and relevant for ordinary people.

Once this initial assignment is completed, men should begin to keep their ears open and eyes alert to other must-read books on the intersection of faith and culture. A man who does not read a book a month is a man whose mind is sorely impoverished. Never go to sleep without a good book at your bedside table.[31] Never step into the car without a good book downloaded on your phone.

7 – Write a Christian Life Plan

The goal of a life plan is alignment: for daily habits to coordinate with ultimate purposes. Therefore, life planning is a version of orienteering. To write a plan is to identify (1) where I am; (2) where

---

31. Men who think they have no time to read need to read the life story of the famous Western novelist, Louis L'Amour who found time to read scores of books while working odd jobs during the Great Depression. See Louis L'Amour, *Education of a Wandering Man* (New York: Random House, 2008).

I need to be; and (3) the key landmarks in-between. To do this, consider where God might have you in six months, in three years, and at the end of life. Look back on how God has led you thus far. Also, take stock of the resources and areas of responsibility that God has given you. The question you need to ask relentlessly is this: how can I steward my gifts and opportunities to serve best the Lord Jesus? The goal of engaging in this exercise is not to outline an immovable itinerary, but to develop a sense of calling. This sense of calling is vital for focusing energy and avoiding distraction.

8 – Persist in the Fundamentals

The means of grace are called means of grace for a reason. They are appointed channels by which God regularly feeds grace into the hearts of believers. If a man is thirsty and walking through the wilderness, the best place to find water is a river. Of course, there is no guarantee that a river will be filled. A drought might occur, leaving the bed dry. Still, a man can be sure that when rain does indeed fall, the first place that water will collect will be in the bed of a river.

The means of grace are like this. They are not automatic. Every gift of God is in fact a gift. Thus the mere act of taking communion does not mean necessarily that grace is conferred. God might have me endure a season of dryness for some higher purpose. Yet, this understood, I can be sure that once the clouds of blessing reappear the first channels through which grace will flow will be the ordinary means of word, sacrament, prayer, and fellowship.

I am repeatedly struck by the relaxed attitude of men regarding the fundamentals of discipleship. Reading the Bible or attending Sunday worship is treated like a spin class, an optional thing to do if a man has spare energy and time. Indeed reading the Bible and church are optional, not in the sense of a spin class, but in the sense of eating food and drinking water. No one has to eat or drink. A person could opt out of food and water at any time. However, the consequences would be life-threatening. The same is true of the core practices of Christian discipleship. They satisfy deep spiritual needs. To ignore them is to ask for trouble.

Practically, what does this mean? *Do the obvious. Persist in the fundamentals.* Start each day right by spending time with God. For a lot of people the beginning of the day is the only time when they are free of interruptions. Get up early enough so that each day you can, like George Mueller, make your heart 'happy' before God.[32]

Furthermore, start each week right. Nothing recalibrates the Christian heart like gathered worship. On Sunday morning we are reminded of the lordship of Christ, the grace of God, and the fellowship of believers. To skip such worship is like skipping oil changes for your car. You might get away with doing it once or twice. However, make a habit of negligence and a severe breakdown will occur.

Final Word

Years ago, when I was still a teenager, I had the opportunity to sit down and have coffee with an older Christian man whom I deeply admired. I remember being nervous about the meeting and writing down a list of questions. At the top of the list, was the following,

---

32. Mueller writes: 'I saw more clearly than ever that the first great and primary business to which I ought to attend every day was to have my soul happy in the Lord. The first thing to be concerned about was not how much I might serve the Lord, or how I might glorify Him, but how I might get my soul into a happy state.' The quote is found in Roger Steer, *Spiritual Secrets of George Mueller* (Wheaton: Harold Shaw, 1985), p. 60.

'How can a young man consecrate his life fully to God?' I couldn't wait to hear my role model's answer.

I won't retell the full conversation. All I will say is that I left feeling frustrated. The question had been misunderstood. The older man had thought that I was a young man struggling to accept the gift of God's grace. I was not. I knew and loved the doctrines of grace. My question was motivated by a desire to pursue wholeheartedly the God who had saved me. I wasn't interested in self-attained righteousness. I was hungry for genuine holiness. I wanted to know God.

I share this story in order to frame the advice in this book. This book is the path that I wish an older Christian had pointed out to me when I was a younger man. I have no doubt that there are other men who hunger and thirst for righteousness, but who lack a sense of direction. In God's grace, my prayer is that the outcome of reading this, more than in anything else, will be clarity regarding the way forward.

Our itinerary is now complete. We have looked at the problem. We have looked at the solution. We have looked at the plan. My job is finished. Yours has just begun.

> *Go, labour on; spend, and be spent,*
> *Thy joy to do the Father's will:*
> *It is the way the Master went;*
> *Should not the servant tread it still?*
>
> *Go, labour on; 'tis not for nought,*
> *Thy earthly loss is heavenly gain:*
> *Men heed thee, love thee, praise thee not;*
> *The Master praises; what are men!*

– HORATIUS BONAR

Church – Do I Have to Go?
by J. Garrett Kell

Church can sometimes be an intimidating thing. It can look like a building full of perfect people who have perfect lives. Not a place where someone who has messed up belongs. But that's not true. The Church is God's people who meet together because they love and need God, and love and need each other. Garrett Kell explains what the Church is, and why it matters whether we go or not.

ISBN: 978-1-5271-0426-6

Character – How Do I Change?
by Sharon Dickens

So, you've heard the Gospel, you've accepted Jesus as your saviour, you're going to Church regularly – you're definitely a Christian, but you don't feel like you're acting like one. The other Christians you know all seem to have it together but how do you get to that point? Even though none of us will be perfect in this life, we can grow to be more and more like Jesus. This book will tell you how.

ISBN: 978-1-5271-0101-2

Training – How Do I Grow as a Christian?
by Isaac Adams

The Christian life is many things, so it can be hard to know how exactly we should live it. Training is a guide to show new Christians just that—how you should live and grow. Walking through the basic spiritual disciplines, Training uses short stories to show how you can love God and your neighbor. What does it look like to follow Jesus, listen to God, talk to God, love your spiritual family and love the lost? That's what this book is all about.

ISBN: 978-1-5271-0102-9

Believe – What Should I Know?
by Mike McKinley

The Bible isn't just a big book full of stories from a long time ago. It also tells us what we are to believe about God, life and what happens after this life. Christians sometimes use a lot of complicated words to describe these things, but this brief breakdown of everything you need to know is easy to understand.

ISBN: 978-1-5271-0305-4

Christian Focus Publications

Our mission statement –

STAYING FAITHFUL

In dependence upon God we seek to impact the world through literature faithful to His infallible Word, the Bible. Our aim is to ensure that the Lord Jesus Christ is presented as the only hope to obtain forgiveness of sin, live a useful life and look forward to heaven with Him.

Our books are published in four imprints:

CHRISTIAN
FOCUS

Popular works including biographies, commentaries, basic doctrine and Christian living.

CHRISTIAN
HERITAGE

Books representing some of the best material from the rich heritage of the church.

MENTOR

Books written at a level suitable for Bible College and seminary students, pastors, and other serious readers. The imprint includes commentaries, doctrinal studies, examination of current issues and church history.

CF4•K

Children's books for quality Bible teaching and for all age groups: Sunday school curriculum, puzzle and activity books; personal and family devotional titles, biographies and inspirational stories – because you are never too young to know Jesus!

Christian Focus Publications Ltd,
Geanies House, Fearn, Ross-shire,
IV20 1TW, Scotland, United Kingdom.
www.christianfocus.com
blog.christianfocus.com

Printed in the United States
By Bookmasters